A Dictionary of the European Communities

Geoffrey Parker
Brenda Parker

Butterworths
London Boston Sydney Wellington Durban Toronto

First published 1981

British Library Cataloguing in Publication Data

Parker, Geoffrey
A dictionary of the European Communities
1. European Economic Community – Dictionaries
I. Title II. *Parker,* Brenda
328.9′142′03 HC241.2

ISBN 0-408-10733-2
ISBN 0-408-10732-4 Pbk

Photoset by Butterworths Litho Preparation Department

Printed in England by
Billing & Sons Ltd., London & Guildford

Preface

This dictionary is intended for the use of all who have an interest in the affairs of the European Communities. Students will find it of particular value in supplementing other sources of information and those engaged in business with the countries of the Continent will also find it a useful reference work. Those having a lively interest in contemporary affairs will find in it an aid to fuller understanding. Entries cover all aspects of Community affairs, past and present, and there are brief biographies of those who have been of greatest importance in the promotion and development of the European Communities and of European unity generally.

There is a widespread tendency to think of the organization as being a unitary one, and, indeed, over the years it has tended to become more so. However, it still consists legally of three separate entities, these being the European Coal and Steel Community, the European Economic Community and the European Atomic Energy Community. The correct collective title is therefore 'The European Communities' and consequently this and the abbreviation E.C. is used throughout the dictionary. When the abbreviation E.E.C. is used specific reference to the European Economic Community is intended. The singular 'European Community' is used only as a general name for the whole group and for the territory which it covers. There are large individual entries for each of the three Communities, for the four major institutions and for the Treaties of Paris and Rome, and it has not been considered necessary or desirable to cross-reference each of these every time they appear in the text.

Finally the authors wish to express their gratitude to the Information Services of the European Communities in Brussels, Luxembourg and London and to the London Embassies of the E.C. member countries. Great care has been taken to check all facts contained in the dictionary but the authors take full responsibility for any faults or errors.

Geoffrey Parker
Brenda Parker

Lichfield 1981

A

Accession, Treaties of

The treaties by which new member states have joined the Community. The Treaties of Accession of the United Kingdom, Ireland, Denmark and Norway were signed in Brussels in 1971. They were subsequently ratified by all the national parliaments, except for that of Norway, and the other three became members in 1973. The treaty of Accession of Greece was signed in Athens in 1978, was subsequently ratified by all the national parliaments, and the country became the tenth member in 1981.

Adenauer, Dr Konrad (1876 – 1967)

Former Chancellor of the Federal Republic of Germany. Born in Cologne and educated at the Universities of Freiburg, Munich and Bonn. Entered politics as a member of the Centre Party before the First World War and became Chief Burgomaster of Cologne in 1917. Removed by the Nazis in 1933 and imprisoned on two occasions. After the Second World War he was one of the founders of the Christian Democrat Party and in 1949 became the Chancellor of the Federal Republic of Germany, remaining in office until 1963. For a period he was also Foreign Minister. His policy was to orientate his country towards the West and he was a great protagonist of European unity. He convinced the Western powers that Germany was of more use to them as a friend than as an ex-enemy and gained German membership of the North Atlantic Treaty Organization (q.v.) and the Organization for European Economic Cooperation (q.v.), the latter contributing to German post-war recovery. He accepted the Schuman Plan (q.v.) and Germany became a founder member of the European Coal and Steel Community and the European Economic Community. One of his greatest achievements was to promote the reconciliation of West Germany and France, and a treaty of cooperation was signed in 1963 between the two countries. He received the Charlemagne Prize (q.v.) in 1954.

African, Caribbean and Pacific (A.C.P.) Countries

Countries signatory to the Lomé Conventions (q.v.). The 57 participants to the renewal of the Convention in 1979 were as follows: Africa–Benin, Botswana, Burundi, Cameroon, Cape Verde Islands, Central African Republic, Chad, Comoros, Congo, Djibouti, Equatorial Guinea. Ethiopia, Gabon, Gambia, Ghana, Guinea, Guinea Bissau, Ivory Coast, Kenya, Lesotho, Liberia, Madagascar, Malawi, Mali, Mauritania, Mauritius, Niger, Nigeria, Rwanda, São Tomé and Principe, Senegal, Seychelles, Sierra Leone, Somalia, Sudan, Swaziland, Tanzania, Togo, Uganda, Upper Volta, Zaire, Zambia.

Caribbean – Bahamas, Barbados, Dominica, Grenada, Guyana, Jamaica, Santa Lucia, Surinam, Trinidad and Tobago.

Pacific – Fiji, Papua-New Guinea, the Solomon Islands, Tonga, Tuvalu, Western Samoa.

Kiribati, St. Vincent and the Grenadines, and Zimbabwe have since also signed the Convention.

Agriculture *see* Common Agricultural Policy

'Agriculture 1980' *see* Mansholt Plan

Alcohol, duty on *see* Excise Duty

Algeria
North African state signatory of the Maghreb cooperation agreements (q.v.). A former French colony which became independent in 1962 but did not join the Yaoundé Convention (q.v.). Specific quotas are laid down for the export to the Community of certain Algerian products covered by the Common Agricultural Policy (q.v.).

Andean Group
A Latin American economic association, the members of which are Bolivia, Colombia, Ecuador, Peru and Venezuela. Contacts have been taking place since 1979 between Andean and the E.C. with a view to establishing closer economic relations. *See also* Latin America, relations with

Andriessen, Frans
Member of the Commission. Born Utrecht 1929 and educated at the University of Utrecht. Entered politics in 1958 as a member of the Utrecht Provincial Estates. Elected Catholic People's Party member of the Dutch Parliament in 1967 and held office as Minister of Finance. Became a member of the Senate in 1980. Appointed Commissioner in 1981 with special responsibility for competition policy.

Argentina
South American country signatory of non-preferential commercial treaty with the E.C. This is renewable annually and there is a special agreement on certain meat exports to the Community.

Arusha Conventions
Agreements signed between the E.C. and the three East African states of Kenya, Uganda and Tanzania closely modelled on the Yaoundé Convention (q.v.). The first Convention was in 1968, but this did not enter into force. The second was in 1969 and operated for a five year term from 1971 on. Under the Convention a free trade area was established between the three countries and the E.C. It did not include agricultural products except for tinned pineapple, coffee and cloves. Special agreements were made for exports of beef and veal, fruit and vegetables, raw tobacco, maize and processed cereals. The agreement was supervised by an Association Council and there was also a joint Parliamentary Committee. The Convention was not renewed and the three states signed the Lomé Convention (q.v.) in 1975.

Assembly of Western European Union *see* Western European Union

Associated African States and Madagascar (A.A.S.M.)
The 18 signatories of the Yaoundé Conventions (q.v.). After Mauritius joined, the group became known as the A.A.S.M.M. The signatories in 1969 were Benin, Burundi, Cameroon, Central African Republic, Chad, Congo-Brazzaville, Gabon, Ivory Coast, Madagascar, Mali, Mauritania, Niger, Rwanda, Senegal, Somalia, Togo, Upper Volta, and Zaire. Mauritius became a signatory in 1973. All these states signed the Lomé Convention (q.v.) in 1975.

Association of South East Asian Nations (A.S.E.A.N.)
Established in 1967 by Indonesia, Thailand, the Philippines, Malaysia and Singapore for the purpose of increasing the economic development and stability of the region. Cooperation takes place at political, economic, social and cultural levels. In 1980 a treaty was signed between the E.C. and A.S.E.A.N. by which the group benefits from the Community's Generalized System of Preferences (*see* Lomé Conventions) and receives financial and technical assistance.

Athens, Treaty of *see* Accession, Treaties of

Australia
There is no trade agreement between the E.C. and Australia, but close contacts are maintained. The Community has an interest in maintaining access to Australia's considerable natural resources, and Australia in turn wishes to maintain its agricultural exports to the Community on a level at least similar to that which prevailed in the United Kingdom market before the latter's accession to the Community.

Austria

Neutral Central European state signatory in 1973 of an industrial free trade agreement with the E.C. This was implemented over a period of years. Member of the European Free Trade Association (q.v.) and the trade agreement followed the enlargement of the Community to include two E.F.T.A. members. Austria's economic relations with the Community are close and the latter is responsible for over a half of her external trade. There is a transit agreement for Community goods crossing Austrian territory. Membership has never been a possibility for Austria since the treaty of 1955, ending the post-war occupation of the country, committed her to a policy of neutrality.

B

Bahamas, The
Caribbean state signatory of the Lomé Conventions (q.v.). Former British colony which became independent in 1973 and is now a member of the Commonwealth.

Barbados
Caribbean state signatory of the Lomé Conventions (q.v.). Former British colony which became independent in 1966 and is now a member of the Commonwealth.

Barcelona Convention
Entered into force in 1976 for the protection of the Mediterranean Sea against marine pollution. The E.C. is one of the signatories.

Barre, Raymond
Former member of the Commission (q.v.). Born Réunion 1924. Studied at the Faculty of Law and the Institut d' Etudes Politiques in Paris. Lecturer at the Institut des Hautes Etudes in Tunis and subsequently at the Universities of Caen and Paris. Member of French government bodies concerned with economic planning, regional development, manpower costs and research. Member and Vice-President of the Commission 1967 to 1972, with responsibility for economic and financial affairs. Author of the Barre Plan (q.v.). French Prime Minister from 1976 to 1981.

Barre Plan
The Commission memorandum and subsequent draft directive of 1969 outlining the means for achieving more effective coordination of national economic policies. In 1970 the Council established the machinery for short-term policy consultation.

Basic price
Price laid down for pigmeat under the Common Agricultural Policy corresponding to the guide price (q.v.) and the target price (q.v.) for other commodities.

'Basket of currencies'
The system by which the value of the European Currency Unit (E.C.U.) (q.v.) is made up of proportions of the different national currencies in the E.C. The weighting of each currency in the 'basket' is related to its current international value.

Bech, Joseph (1887 – 1975)
Former Prime Minister and Foreign Minister of Luxembourg. Born Diekirch, Luxembourg and entered politics in 1914. Minister of Foreign Affairs from 1926 to 1944 and Prime Minister from 1953 to 1958 during which time he also held the office of Foreign Minister. Active protagonist of European unity who was chairman of the Messina Conference (q.v.), a signatory of the Treaty of Rome and a member of the Council of Ministers. Awarded the Charlemagne Prize (q.v.) in 1960.

Beddington-Behrens, Sir Edward (1898 – 1969)
Member of the Secretariat of the League of Nations, founder member of the European Movement (q.v.) and chairman of its British

Council. Enthusiastic advocate of British membership of the Community.

Beef and Veal
Production and trade in these commodities is subject to the regulations of the Common Agricultural Policy (q.v.). Guide prices are fixed annually, the support measures being intervention buying and private storage aids. These come into action when prices fall below a given level. Birth premiums for calves and slaughter premiums for cattle are granted at the discretion of authorities in each member state, and there may be limited sales of beef at reduced prices to dispose of surplus stocks. A variable import levy takes account of the difference between the guide price (q.v.) and the frontier offer price. Refunds to exporters of the difference between the Community and world prices are granted where applicable.

B.E.I. (Banque Européenne d'Investissement) *see* European Investment Bank

Belgium
Founder member state of the European Community and member of most other Western European and Atlantic organizations. Area 30500 km^2 and population (1978) 9.8 millions, giving a density of 322 per km^2 which, after the Netherlands, is the highest in the Community. The modern Belgian state dates from 1831 when it was established after a revolution against Dutch rule imposed at the Congress of Vienna. Belgian independence was subsequently guaranteed by the Treaty of London in 1839. In the later nineteenth century Belgium acquired a large African empire known as the Belgian Congo. This achieved independence in 1960, taking the name of Zaire (q.v.). Belgium is a monarchy (Head of State: King Baudouin) and a parliamentary democracy which until recently has had a fairly centralized state structure on the model of France. Within its frontiers it contains a number of linguistic groups, the most significant being the Dutch-speaking Flemings in the north and the French-speaking Walloons in the south. There has been considerable friction between these two groups, and a system of devolved regional government on a linguistic basis is now being introduced.

While the country has only 2 per cent of the Community's total area and 4 per cent of its population, it is in reality a far more significant member than these percentages would suggest. It accounts for some 5 per cent of the Community's G.D.P. and 10 per cent of its external trade. It is an intensely developed industrial and trading country, 38 per cent of the population being engaged in industry while only 3 per cent are now in agriculture. Modern Belgian heavy industry grew up on the southern coalfield, but this has now decreased in importance and much of the country's industrial development since the Second World War has taken place in the Fleming north. The older industrial regions of Wallonia have experienced considerable difficulties and have received large amounts of both national and Community aid. The capital city, Brussels (q.v.), is the home of the Commission and the Council of Ministers and the major centre of E.C. bureaucracy. Since 1922 Belgium has been associated with Luxembourg in the Belgo-Luxembourg Economic Union (q.v.).

Belgo-Luxembourg Economic Union (B.L.E.U.)
This organization first came into existence in 1922 in response to the political and economic conditions prevailing after the First World War. Luxembourg (q.v.), recognizing that total economic independence was unrealistic for a country of her size, and not desiring close association with Germany, entered into a union with Belgium. It provides for complete freedom of trade between the two countries together with a currency alignment and joint financial arrangements. This has effectively integrated Luxembourg into the Belgian economy and has been an essential part of the country's economic life since then. B.L.E.U. was the precursor of similar international economic arrangements including the E.C. itself.

Benelux countries *see* Belgium, Netherlands, Luxembourg

Benelux Memorandum
Originally conceived by Johan Beyen, the Dutch foreign minister, and submitted jointly by the governments of the Benelux countries in 1955 for consideration by the Messina Conference (q.v.). It advocated the integration of certain specific sectors within an overall economic community. It was influential in getting the Conference to accept the

principle of broader economic integration and the Spaak Committee was given the task of drawing up the plans for the implementation of this. *See also* Spaak Report.

Benelux Union
Institutionalization of close economic ties between Belgium, the Netherlands and Luxembourg. It is based on a convention signed by the three countries in London in 1944 which came into effect in 1947. It established a customs union and promoted the development of closer relations. A full economic union which provided for the movement of labour and capital came into force in 1960. While basically economic in method, the Union was also originally intended to add to the strength of three relatively small and vulnerable countries which had suffered during the Second World War. Together they have a population of 24 millions and a G.D.P. about equal to that of Italy. While Benelux still maintains an individual identity, its policies have increasingly been merged with those of the E.C. as a whole.

Benin
West African state signatory of the Yaoundé and Lomé Conventions (q.v.). Formerly the French colony of Dahomey, it became independent in 1960 and took its present name in 1975.

Berlaymont, Bâtiment, Rue de la Loi, 200, Brussels
Headquarters of the Commission of the European Communities (q.v.). Opened in 1969, it dominates the city's 'Community quarter.' It was financed and built by the Belgian government, and is on lease to the E.C.

Berlin
The capital city of Germany until the end of the Second World War in 1945. Germany was then divided by the victorious powers into four zones occupied respectively by Great Britain, France, the United States and the Soviet Union. While Berlin fell within the Soviet zone, it had been agreed at the Yalta Conference that the capital itself would also be divided into four zones so that the powers would each have a presence there. The city's affairs were run by a joint four-power military administration, but difficulties were caused by the increasing estrangement of the three western powers from the Soviet Union. In 1948 the Soviet Union cut off land communications to the three western zones, and the city was kept going only by a massive Anglo-American airlift. When agreement was at last reached the city had become effectively divided into two zones, the Soviet and the western, and the progressive isolation of the latter was later made almost total by the construction of the Berlin Wall by the Communists in 1961. While East Berlin became the capital of the German Democratic Republic (q.v.), the ties of West Berlin (q.v.) were increasingly with the Federal Republic of Germany (q.v.) and the rest of the western world. The situation was given a form of international legal status by the four-power agreements of 1972.

Berne Convention
Entered into force in 1963 for the protection of the Rhine against chemical pollution. The E.C. is one of the signatories.

B.E.U.C.
Bureau Européen des Unions Consommateurs *see* European Bureau of Consumer Unions

Bevin, Ernest (1881 – 1951)
British foreign secretary from 1945 to 1951. Encouraged close British involvement with organizations established to unite and strengthen the western nations in the aftermath of the Second World War and to combat the apparent threat posed by the Soviet Union. However, he opposed the early efforts to involve Britain more closely in the establishment of a united Europe on the grounds that this would have weakened ties with the Commonwealth and the United States.

Biesheuvel, Barend William
Dutch political leader. Born Haarlemerliede in 1920 and educated at Amsterdam University. Entered politics in 1957 and held office as Minister of Agriculture and Fisheries and Deputy Prime Minister. Leader of the Anti-Revolutionary Party in the Dutch parliament since 1967. Member of the European Parliament from 1963 to 1979 and one of the 'Three Wise Men' (q.v.).

Birklebach Report
Report, named after its German author, submitted to the European Parliament in 1963 on the problems of regional imbalance in the Community. It pointed out the great concentrations of economic activity and population which had grown up in the central areas and the chronic difficulties experienced by the more peripheral ones.

B.L.E.U. *see* Belgo-Luxembourg Economic Union

Bonn
Capital city of the Federal Republic of Germany (West Germany) since the latter was established in 1949. A relatively small town (Population 150 000) located just to the south of Cologne. It was chosen as a symbol of the new start for Germany after the defeat of 1945 and of the dimished role of central government in the affairs of the new federal state.

Bonn Convention
Community Convention proposed in 1976 for the prevention of chemical pollution of the Rhine. Agreed by Council but not formally adopted. *See also* Berne Convention.

Borschette, Albert (1920 – 1974)
Former member of the Commission. Born Diekirch and educated at the Universities of Aix-en-Provence, Munich, Erlangen and Paris. Entered government service in 1945 and served in Brussels, Berlin and Bonn. Permanent representative of Luxembourg to the European Communities from 1958 to 1970. Commissioner from 1970 to 1974 in charge of competition and personnel.

Botswana
Southern African state signatory of the Lomé Conventions (q.v.). Formerly the British protectorate of Bechuanaland which became independent in 1966 and is now a republic within the Commonwealth.

Brandt, Willy
Born Lubeck 1913. German Social Democratic statesmen active in the resistance against the Third Reich during the Second World War. Mayor of West Berlin from 1957 to 1966 and subsequently Federal German Minister of Foreign Affairs from 1966 to 1969. Federal German Chancellor from 1969 to 1974. Particularly identified with the improvements in relations between West Germany and the countries of eastern Europe known as the 'ostpolitik.' This entailed for the first time German official recognition of the post-war boundaries in eastern Europe, and treaties were signed with Poland and the Soviet Union in 1972. Brandt was always an active supporter of the European Community and a strong protagonist of British membership in the late 1960s. A Socialist member of the European Parliament since 1979.

Brazil
South American state signatory of a non-preferential commercial treaty with the E.C. As part of this there is a joint committee on cooperation in scientific, technical, agricultural and energy matters.

Briand, Aristide (1862 – 1932)
French statesman who held the office of Prime Minister and Foreign Minister on a number of occasions. Supporter of the League of Nations and active in promoting a new spirit of understanding and cooperation between France and Germany in the 1920s. Awarded the Nobel Peace Prize jointly with Gustav Stresemann (q.v.) in 1926. Author of the Briand Plan (q.v.).

Briand Plan, The
Proposal by Aristide Briand (q.v.) in 1930 for the setting up of a European Union. It envisaged a 'united states of Europe' with a federal government reponsible in the first instance mainly for economic affairs. The idea received much support from the smaller nations, but less from the more powerful. The United Kingdom, whose influence at the time was considerable, was unenthusiastic and the scheme had to be quietly dropped.

Britain *see* United Kingdom

Brugmans, Hendrik
Distinguished writer and academic. Born 1906 in Amsterdam. Educated Paris and Amsterdam Universities. Socialist member of the Dutch Parliament and member of the Resistance during the Second World War. Re-entered politics in 1945 and became the first president of the Europcan Federalist Union. Rector of the College of Europe, Bruges (q.v.) from 1950 to 1972. Awarded the Charlemagne Prize (q.v.) in 1951.

Brunner, Guido
Former member of the Commission. Born 1930 in Madrid. Official in the German Ministry of Foreign Affairs since 1955. Leader of the German delegation to the Conference on Security and Cooperation in Europe (C.S.C.E.) in Helsinki and the second stage of the Geneva Conference. Member of the Commission from 1974 to 1980 in charge of energy, research, science and education.

Brussels
Capital of Belgium and, with a popluation of 1.1 million, the largest and most important city in the country. It is a major commercial, industrial and cultural centre well located in relation to the country's main geographical and linguistic regions. It constitutes a French-speaking enclave in the middle of the Dutch-speaking countryside slightly to the north of the country's main Fleming – Walloon linguistic divide. Both French and Dutch (Flemish) are official languages and other European languages are also now widely spoken. In 1958 the city was chosen to be the headquarters of the newly-established European Economic Community and the associated European Atomic Energy Community. With the merger of these two Communities with the European Coal and Steel Community in 1968, Brussels gained pre-eminence as the principal centre of Community activities. It contains the main offices of the Commission and Council of Ministers and some 7000 of the 11 000 staff employed by the Commission now work there. It also has the headquarters of many other international organizations, pre-eminent among them being the North Atlantic Treaty Organization (q.v.) which moved from Paris in 1969 at the time of the French withdrawal. As a result of all these developments, together with the inflow of immigrant workers, Brussels is now a highly cosmopolitan city and 28 per cent of its total population is non-Belgian.

Brussels, Treaty of
Treaty signed in 1948 by France, the United Kingdom, Belgium, the Netherlands and Luxembourg which established the Brussels Treaty Organization for a period of fifty years. Each of the five countries undertook to go to the aid of any one of their number which was the object of an armed attack in Europe by a third country. It also established the machinery for the coordination of foreign policies and for cooperation in the economic, social and cultural fields. In 1955 the Federal Republic of Germany and Italy were admitted and the organization was renamed Western European Union (q.v.).

Budget, Annual Community
This consists of the total projected expenditure by the European Communities in any one year. In 1979 it amounted to 14 000 million EUA (q.v.) which represents 0.7 per cent of the total GDP of the Communities. The contributions of the member states have been gradually replaced over the years by an 'own resources' system whereby all customs duties and agricultural levies go direct to the E.C. and the remainder is mainly made up by an agreed proportion of VAT (q.v.). The budget is drawn up initially by the Commission. It consists of two parts, the compulsory expenditure entailed in previously agreed policies and non-compulsory expenditure for funding new developments. The budget is presented to the Council which considers it and then sends it on to the European Parliament. The latter has the duty to consider it and to propose any modifications or amendments within an agreed period. It is subsequently returned to Council which considers any changes made by Parliament and votes by a qualified majority on acceptance or rejection. The budget is then returned to Parliament which adopts it unless it is rejected by an absolute majority of members or two-thirds of the votes actually cast. The most important sectors of E.C. budgetary expenditure are agriculture which alone has two-thirds of the total, regional aid, social and training schemes, aid to developing countries and research into such matters as energy sources, transport and industrial modernization.

Budget Policy Committee
The Committee of the European Parliament allocated the task of scrutinizing the Annual Community Budget.

Burke, Richard
Former member of the Commission. Born 1932 in New York. Elected to the Dáil Eireann in 1969 as a Fine Gael member. Minister of Education from 1973 to 1976. Commissioner from 1977 to 1980 with responsibility for taxation, consumer affairs, transport and relations with the European Parliament.

Burundi
Central African state signatory of the Yaoundé and Lomé Conventions (q.v.). Formerly the Belgian trusteeship territory of Urundi, it became independent in 1962.

Business Cooperation Centre
This was set up by the Commission in 1972 in order to promote greater cooperation among companies in different member states. Known as the 'marriage bureau,' it supplies information and arranges contacts between companies wishing to enter into cooperation arrangements or mergers. Its appeal has been largely to middle-sized firms interested in extending their international operations and it has achieved considerable success.

Butter
Product subject to price regulation under the Common Agricultural Policy (q.v.). If necessary, levies are imposed on imports to bring prices up to the Community's target price (q.v.). Aid is provided for private storage of unsold stocks and, if necessary, these may be disposed of through reduced prices to food manufacturers and certain categories of consumers. A general consumer subsidy may employ a certain proportion of the Finance of the European Agricultural Guidance and Guarantee Fund (q.v.). Export refunds are available when world prices are below the Community target price. Accumulated butter stocks may be disposed of through low price bulk sales, particularly to Eastern Europe.

'Butter mountain'
Stocks of unsold butter accumulated as a result of intervention buying by the European Agricultural Guidance and Guarantee Fund (q.v.).

C

Cameroon
West African state signatory of the Yaoundé and Lomé Conventions (q.v.). Formerly consisting of two United Nations trust territories administered by the United Kingdom and France, it became independent and a Federal Republic in 1961.

Cape Verde Islands
Island state off the west coast of Africa signatory of the Lomé Conventions (q.v.). Former Portuguese colony which became independent in 1975.

Cardiff
Capital city and largest town in Wales and location of the E.C. Welsh office.

Central African Republic
Central African state signatory of the Yaoundé and Lomé Conventions (q.v.). Former French colony of Ubangi Shari, it became independent in 1958. Between 1976 and 1979 it was styled the Central African Empire.

C.E.R.N.
Centre Européenne pour la Récherche Nucléaire *see* European Centre for Nuclear Research.

Chad
Central African state signatory of the Yaoundé and Lomé Conventions (q.v.). Former French colony which became independent in 1958.

Channel Tunnel project
Discussed for many years by the British and French governments, Britain's entry into the Community and increased orientation towards Europe gave it greater urgency. In 1979 the Commission came out in favour of the project and proposed the use of Community funds to help finance it. The Commission considered that it would be likely to have a positive effect on the economies of the adjacent regions.

Charlemagne Prize
Awarded annually since 1949 by the West German city of Aachen for outstanding contributions to European unity and international cooperation. The first recipient was Count Richard Coudenhove-Kalergi, and others have included Hendrik Brugmans, Alcide de Gasperi, Jean Monnet, Konrad Adenauer, Winston Churchill, Paul-Henri Spaak, Robert Schuman, Walter Hallstein, Edward Heath and Roy Jenkins. *See* appropriate entries in the dictionary for further information on individual recipients.

Cheese
Product subject to price regulation under the Common Agricultural Policy (q.v.). Levies are imposed as necessary on imports to bring prices to the Community's target price (q.v.). Aid is available for the private storage of unsold stocks, and export refunds may be made when world prices are below the E.C. target price.

Cheysson, Claude
Former member of the Commission. Born Paris in 1920 and educated at the Ecole Polytechnique, Ecole Normale Supérieure and Ecole Nationale d'Administration. Entered the French civil service, becoming secretary to the Minister of Foreign Affairs and later *chef de cabinet* to the Prime Minister, Pierre Mendès-France. Subsequently counsellor in the Ministry of Foreign Affairs, Secretary-General of the Commission for Technical Cooperation in Africa and Director-General of the Technical Organisation for the Exploitation of Sahara Minerals. From 1966 to 1970 he was French ambassador to Indonesia. Commissioner from 1973 to 1981 with special responsibility for aid and development. Cheysson negotiated the Lomé Convention (q.v.), and its subsequent renewal. Appointed French Foreign Minister in 1981.

'Chicken war'
Dispute between the E.C. and the United States during the 1960s over American exports of poultry to the Community. The level of these was restricted in accordance with the Common Agricultural Policy (q.v.) and the result was a period of strained economic relations and accusations by the Americans that the Community's agricultural policy was too protectionist.

Christian Democrats *see* European People's Party

Churchill, Sir Winston Spencer (1874–1965)
Grandson of the 7th Duke of Marlborough, born Blenheim Palace and educated at Harrow and Sandhurst. Commissioned and served in India and Africa. Entered politics in 1900 as Conservative M.P. for Oldham, but joined the Liberal party in 1904 over the Free Trade issue. Became Home Secretary and later First Lord of the Admiralty until 1915. In the 1920s he rejoined the Conservatives and was Chancellor of the Exchequer from 1924 to 1929. In 1939 he once more became First Lord of the Admiralty and from 1940 to 1945 led the coalition government which brought the Second World War to a successful conculsion. Following electoral defeat in 1945 he concerned himself with strengthening the will of the western world to resist the Soviet Union, and gave encouragement to the movement for a united Europe. His Zurich speech of 1946 is a landmark in the process of post-war reconciliation. He was present at the Hague Conference (q.v.) and for a time was a member of the Council of Europe (q.v.). Yet on becoming Prime Minister for the second time from 1951 to 1955 he failed to make any new European initiatives. Churchill was at heart an imperialist and did not regard Britain as being really a part of Europe. Although enthusiastic about the idea of a 'united states of Europe,' he saw Britain and the British Commonwealth as being ranked among its 'friends and sponsors.' Britain, in his view, would choose 'the open sea' in preference to Europe, and this was to have a considerable effect on European attitudes to future British participation. Awarded the Charlemagne Prize (q.v.) in 1956.

College of Europe, Bruges
Established in 1950 for the study of Europe and European integration. Intended for post-graduates who come from all over Europe to pursue courses in their chosen fields of study. The College contains the European Study Centre for the Preservation of the Architectural and Urban Heritage.

Colombo, Emilio
Italian political leader. Born 1920 and educated Rome University. Entered politics in 1946 as a Christian Democrat member of the Constituent Assembly, and subsequently held most of the great offices of state including that of Prime Minister. Member of the European Parliament from 1976 until direct elections in 1979, during most of which time he served as President. Italian Minister of Foreign Affairs in 1980.

Comecon *see* Council for Mutual Economic Assistance

Commission, The
The executive body of the European Communities. The Commission of the European Economic Community was established in 1958 under the institutional provisions of the Treaties of Rome. It had nine members, two each from France, the Federal Republic of Germany and Italy and one each from Belgium, the Netherlands and Luxembourg. A similar Commission was established to take charge of the European Atomic Energy Community. In 1968 the two Commissions,

together with the High Authority of the European Coal and Steel Community were merged and a joint Commission consisting of fourteen members took office until 1970 when a new nine member Commission with responsibility for all three Communities took office. With the enlargement of the Community in 1973, the Commission itself was increased to thirteen members, the United Kingdom having two Commissioners and Denmark and Ireland one each. The entry of Greece in 1981 increased the total number of Commissioners to fourteen. Commissioners chosen for their 'general competence and indisputable independence,' are nominated by the governments of member states and they tend to be drawn from politics, the trade unions and the higher reaches of the civil service. They hold office for periods of four years, being then eligible for reappointment. The President of the Commission is appointed by Council for a two year renewable period, and it has been usual to rotate this office among the member states. Since 1958 the Presidents have been Walter Hallstein (q.v.), Jean Rey (q.v.), Franco Maria Malfatti (q.v.), Sicco Mansholt (q.v.), François-Xavier Ortoli (q.v.), Roy Jenkins (q.v.), and Gaston Thorn (q.v.). There also five Vice-Presidents.

The Commission has responsibility for the day to day running of the E.C. and is in charge of all staff working in Brussels, Luxembourg, Strasbourg and other centres. The power of initiative is vested in it and responsibility for drafting new proposals for consideration by Council.

It is obliged to revise proposals if requested by Council and must take note of the opinion of Parliament. Following Council's legislative decisions the Commission has the duty of implementation and ensuring that they are observed throughout the Community. It is empowered to take governments, firms or other bodies to the Court in the case of alleged infringement of obligations under the Treaties and subsequent legislation. The Commission draws up the annual budget which must then be approved by both Council and Parliament before it can be implemented. It produces an annual report for Parliament on the activities of the E.C. and is required to submit new proposals to the Council when requested to do so. The Commission sits as a cabinet and takes decisions by majority vote. Each Commissioner is allocated his own particular responsibilities and has a staff to help carry these out. During their term of office the Commissioners can only be removed collectively by a two-thirds vote of censure in Parliament or, in special circumstances, individually by the Court. In the early years the Commission had a pre-eminent role in Community affairs, but this diminished following the Luxembourg Agreement (q.v.) in 1966. Since then the central position has been increasingly taken over by the Council of Ministers and the European Council assisted by such bodies as the Committee of Permanent Representatives (q.v.) and the Committee of Political Directors (q.v.). Nevertheless it remains central to the working, if not the policy-making, of the E.C. and is able to exert considerable influence on decisions. The members of the Commission which took office in 1981 were Gaston Thorn; Frans Andriessen; Claude Cheysson; Poul Dalsager; Etienne Davignon; Antonio Giolitti; Wilhelm Haferkamp; George Kontogeorgis; Lorenzo Natali; Karl-Heinz Narjes; Michael O'Kennedy; François-Xavier Ortoli; Ivor Richard; Christopher Tugendhat. Finn Gundelach died shortly after taking office, and Claude Cheysson left the Commission later in 1981 on his appointment as French Foreign Minister. He was replaced by Edgard Pisani (q.v.). *See* individual biographical entries.

Committee of Permanent Representatives (COREPER)
Committee of the ambassadors of member states accredited to the Community. It prepares the work of the Council (q.v.) and carries out related tasks allocated to it. It has become of great importance in preparing the ground for new measures under consideration by the Council.

Committee of Political Directors
Committee consisting of high foreign office officials of the member states for the discussion of common foreign policy questions. The officials are based on their own national capitals, and their principal function is to prepare the ground for the Meetings of Foreign Ministers in Political Cooperation (q.v.).

Common Agricultural Policy (C.A.P.)
This came into being as a result of the decision to include agriculture in the common market established under the Treaty of Rome (q.v.). Owing to the particular physical, economic and historical factors which govern agricultural production, a special system had to be devised which would help

modernize agriculture, ensure supplies to the consumers and give an adequate return to the farmer. In order to accomplish this it was judged necessary to set up a managed market for agricultural produce. The mechanism for this 'green pool' began to operate for cereals in 1962 and has since been extended to cover a whole range of agricultural produce. Target prices are agreed in advance and the mechanism for ensuring that they remain within the agreed band is intervention buying and selling. If the price falls too low, the Community buys produce and puts it into store. Likewise if the price rises too high the commodity it taken out of store and sold. The E.C. agricultural market is protected from the fluctuations of world prices by the Common External Levy (q.v.). The Community funds this operation and also provides aid for modernization of the agricultural sector, the financial instrument for this purpose being the European Agricultural Guidance and Guarantee Fund (q.v.). The C.A.P. offers farmers a very large potential market for their produce and the possibility of much greater specialization. Since C.A.P. was established European agriculture has been completely transformed and the efficiency of large areas has been greatly improved. However, prices have been maintained at high levels, a policy not popular with the consumers and arguably one putting a brake on modernization and innovation. It has certainly contributed to the production of surpluses and these 'mountains' have often had to be disposed of at a loss. The high costs have made the C.A.P. unpopular in many quarters and there have been demands for its reform.

Common Assembly *see* European Parliament

Common Customs Tariff (C.C.T.)
Tariff levied on goods entering the E.C. from third countries excluding agricultural products covered by the common organization of the market (q.v.) which are subject to the Common External Levy (q.v.). The C.C.T. applies equally at all points of entry into the E.C. from third countries, the appropriate level being determined for each product group. It was established over a transitional period simultaneously with the elimination of the internal E.C. tariffs. It was fixed at the average of the national tariffs in operation at the time of the signature of the Treaty of Rome. The C.C.T. became fully operational in the six original members in 1968 and, following the transition period, it was applied to Denmark, Ireland and the United Kingdom by 1977. It is also being progressively applied to Greece. Since 1968 the Council of Ministers has been responsible for determining the levels of the C.C.T. and these reflect the decisions made by the General Agreement on Tariffs and Trade (q.v.).

Common External Levy
This variable levy is charged on agricultural produce entering the Community from third countries when world prices are lower than current E.C. prices. It consists of the difference between the import price and the target price (q.v.) operating within the E.C. and is used for cereals, milk products, sugar and olive oil. For pigmeat, eggs and poultrymeat there is the additional sluicegate price, which is that of the most efficient third country producer and the levy is increased to ensure that nothing is sold at below this price. The purpose of the levy is not to exclude imports, but to protect the Community's agricultural market from disruption caused by low-cost imports. It also provides a source of income which goes directly to the Commission. When E.C. prices are below world prices, the system goes into reverse so as to protect European consumers from shortages.

Common Fisheries Policy
Under the Treaties E.C. member states may take restrictive measures within their own coastal waters. There have been a number of E.C. fishery agreements, including the establishment of a 200 mile fishing zone around the Community's coasts restricted to licenced E.C. fishermen. Concern with the effects of overfishing on stocks has resulted in the institution of quotas for catches of different species and the Commission is responsible for monitoring catches in Community waters and landings at Community ports. The European Agricultural Guidance and Guarantee Fund (q.v.) is empowered to make grants for the improvement of the fishing industry and for aid to areas dependent upon it. *See also* Exclusive Economic Zone.

Common market
A common market is any multinational free trade area protected by a common external tariff. The European Community is a common market of this sort, and it is a name widely used for the organization.

Common organization of the market (C.O.M.)
Collective measures taken under the Common Agricultural Policy (q.v.) to secure levels of production, internal prices and protection of agricultural produce within the Community. Each product has its own C.O.M. appropriate to the particular conditions of production, self-sufficiency and market. Measures taken include import levies, price determination, financial guarantees to farmers and export refunds. *See also* information on individual products.

Commonwealth, The
Loose association of sovereign states which emerged following the granting of independence to the former British dependent territories. Formerly known as the 'British Commonwealth,' it is now mainly a forum for discussion and there are few agreed common policies. Following British membership of the Community in 1973 the special trading relationship based on 'imperial preference' came to an end. In 1975 21 Commonwealth states signed the new Lomé Convention (q.v.), so effectively continuing their preferences in the British market and gaining access to the Community market as well. Trading ties with Britain have often survived the formal end of the special economic relationship, and many Commonwealth countries are still important sources of the country's foodstuffs and raw materials. After 1973 special arrangements were made for the continuation of the export of certain foodstuffs from New Zealand (q.v.). Some Commonwealth states, in particular the more developed ones, have no preferential trade agreements with the E.C. and they have consequently faced problems of access to the Community market.

Communist Group
One of the seven party groups in the European Parliament. In the direct elections of 1979 it won 44 seats. Except for one Dane, all its members are from Italy and France.

Comoros
Island state off the east coast of Africa signatory of the Lomé Convention (q.v.). Former French colony which became independent in 1974.

Competition
The Treaty of Rome requires that no restrictions be placed on free competition within the E.C. and in principle all agreements which restrict competition or distort free trade are prohibited. The only exemptions are agreements which improve production or distribution or have a positive effect on economic and technical progress. The abuse of a dominant position, including state monopoly, is also prohibited. Subsequent Community legislation has given the Commission power to exempt certain agreements on exclusive dealing, patent licensing, subcontracting and agreements tending to further specialization and product research. Certain state aids are also acceptable so long as the aim is to reach a durable solution to structural problems. These rules and guidelines also apply in the transport sector.

Confederation of European Community Family Organizations (C.O.F.A.C.E.)
Organization with headquarters in Brussels for the promotion of the interests and values of the family in the context of social and economic change.

Congo, People's Republic of
Central African state signatory of the Yaoundé and Lomé Conventions (q.v.). Formerly the French colony of Middle Congo, it became independent in 1958.

Consultative Assembly of Council of Europe *see* Council of Europe

Consumers *see* European Bureau of Consumers Unions

Convention on the Conservation of European Wildlife
Signed by the Commission in 1979. This Convention places an obligation on signatories to take the necessary legal and administrative action to protect listed birds, animals, plants and amphibians, and also to protect the natural environments required for their survival.

Coppé, Albert
Former member of the Commission. Born Bruges 1911 and educated at the Catholic University of Louvain. Entered parliament as a member of the Christian Social Party for

Bruges in 1946 and held office successively as Minister of Public Works, Minister of Economic Affairs and Minister of Reconstruction. Vice-President of the High Authority of the European Coal and Steel Community from 1952 until the merger of the Communities in 1967. Member of the Commission from 1967 to 1973, having responsibility between 1967 and 1970 for information, credit and investments and between 1970 and 1973 for social affairs, transport, personnel and administration, credit and investments, budgets and financial control.

Coudenhove-Kalergi, Count Richard (1894 – 1972)
Writer and thinker on European affairs, born in Tokyo 1894. In 1924 founded the Pan-European Union and later won wide support for his ideas on a confederal Europe. Worked closely for a time with Aristide Briand (q.v.) and supported the latter's 'united states of Europe.' After the Second World War he founded the European Parliamentary Union and continued his work for confederal solutions. First recipient of the Charlemagne Prize (q.v.) in 1950.

Council for Mutual Economic Assistance (C.M.E.A.)
Inter-state organization of Socialist countries known popularly as Comecon. It was set up in 1949 by the Soviet Union, Poland, Czechoslovakia, Hungary, Romania, Bulgaria and Albania and joined in 1950 by the German Democratic Republic (q.v.). Since then Mongolia, Cuba and Vietnam have become members and Albania has been expelled. The objects of the organization are to promote economic growth, increase mutual trade and develop common policies. There was much opposition, particularly in Romania, to the implementation of supranational economic policies and many of these subsequently had to be abandoned. Negotiations between the E.C. and Comecon have been in progress since 1974 but there have been considerable difficulties in reaching any agreements partly owing to the differences in the fields of competence of the institutions of the two organizations.

Council of Europe
Established in 1949 in the wake of strong European feeling engendered by the Hague Conference (q.v.). The original member states were the United Kingdom, France, Italy, Belgium, the Netherlands, Luxembourg, Denmark, Norway, Sweden and Ireland. The Council has subsequently been joined by Austria, West Germany, Greece, Cyprus, Iceland, Malta, Switzerland and Turkey. It consists of a Committee of Foreign Ministers and a Consultative Assembly nominated by member governments. The original hope was that it would be the basis for closer European cooperation, but the opposition of certain member states made this impossible. It was the body in which much of the debate on the future of Europe took place prior to the establishment of the European Coal and Steel Community, and subsequently it has been largely a forum for discussion on matters of common concern. It has concerned itself with important questions such as human rights, health, conservation and the protection of the environment and conventions have been produced in many of these areas. When there have been divisions among the countries of western Europe, the Council has been one of the channels for keeping communications open. The Council meets in the Palais de l'Europe in Strasbourg, and this is now used also for meetings of the European Parliament.

Council of Ministers
One of the institutions of the European Communities set up under the Treaties and normally referred to as the Council. There is one minister from each member state, either the foreign minister or the one appropriate to the business being transacted, for instance agriculture, regional policy or energy. Each country holds the presidency for a six month period, the incumbent being responsible for calling meetings as necessary. The Council considers proposals from the Commission and, although it cannot itself amend them, it may return them to the Commission for reconsideration. Decisions are made by either simple majority, qualified majority or unanimity. A qualified majority, as laid down in the Treaties, means in practice that at least six members must give assent to a proposed measure. Unanimity is necessary in accordance with the Luxembourg Agreement (q.v.) for matters considered by any one member state as affecting its 'vital interests.' The Council is the main decision-taking body and the legislative organ of the Community. In legal terms the European Council (q.v.) consists of the heads of state or government meeting as the Council of Ministers.

Culham *see* Joint European Torus; European Schools

Customs Union
Abolition of all restrictions on trade among a group of states and the institution of a common trade policy in relation to third countries. This then results in the creation of a common market (q.v.).

Cyprus
Mediterranean island state and member of the Commonwealth which in 1972 signed an association agreement with the E.C. This provides for the creation of an industrial free trade area between Cyprus and the Community and preferential access for Cypriot agricultural produce into the Community market. There is also provision for financial aid in the form of loans and grants from the European Investment Bank. Since 1974 the northern part of the island has been occupied by Turkish forces and the Community has stated that it finds the partition of the island incompatible with the provisions of the association agreement.

D

Dahomey *see* Benin

Dahrendorf, Professor Ralf
Former member of the Commission. Born Hamburg 1929 and educated Hamburg and London School of Economics. Imprisoned by the Gestapo during the Second World War. At first a Social Democrat but became a Free Democrat member of the Landtag of Baden Württemberg in 1968. Secretary of State for Foreign Affairs in 1969. Commissioner from 1970 to 1974 first with special responsibility for external relations and trade and from 1973 on for research, science, technology, scientific information, the Joint Research Centre (q.v.) and the Statistical Office. Outspoken critic of the diminution in the Commission's role. Resigned in 1974 to become Director of the London School of Economics. Writer on contemporary political and economic affairs.

Dairy products *see* Butter, Cheese, Milk and milk products

Dalsager, Poul
Member of the Commission. Born Hirtshals 1929 and educated in commerce. Career in banking before entering national politics as member of the Danish Parliament in 1964. Was chairman of the parliamentary committee on relations with the European Communities and held office as Minister for Agriculture and Fisheries from 1975 to 1981. Following Danish membership of the E.C. became a member and Vice-President of the European Parliament. Appointed Commissioner with special responsibility for agriculture in 1981 following the death of Finn Gundelach (q.v.).

Dankert, Pieter
Born 1934. Socialist member of the Dutch Parliament, member of the Consultative Assembly of the Council of Europe (q.v.) and the Assembly of Western European Union (q.v.). Member of the European Parliament since 1977 and *rapporteur* of its Budgets Committee from 1979 to 1980.

Davignon Committee
Committee of Community Foreign Ministers named after Viscount Etienne Davignon (q.v.) which reported in 1970 on the coordination of foreign policy. Since 1973 the Ministers have met on a regular basis for the specific purpose of considering foreign policy questions. When in session for this purpose they are known as Meetings of Foreign Ministers in Political Cooperation (q.v.).

Davignon, Etienne, Viscount
Member of the Commission. Born Budapest 1932, educated in Budapest and subsequently moved to Belgium where he became a civil servant in the cabinet office. From 1964 he was *chef de cabinet* first to Paul Spaak and then to Pierre Harmel. Moved to the E.C. in 1969 as Director-General for Policy and in 1974 became chairman of the Governing Board of the International Energy Agency.

Commissioner since 1977 in charge of internal market and industrial affairs, and from 1981 also of energy and research policy. At a period of crisis for the Community's industry, his approach has been interventionist and he was the originator of the Davignon Plan (q.v.) for the rescue of the steel industry.

Davignon Plan
Commission plan for the Community's steel industry named after Etienne Davignon (q.v.), Commissioner in charge of industrial affairs from 1977. It aims to deal with the crisis in the industry which began in 1974 resulting from the overcapacity built up by the high levels of investment in the 1960s, decreased demand for steel because of the economic recession, and competition from overseas producers. The plan aims in the short term to put ceilings on production capacity, tighten anti-dumping measures and discipline trade. In the longer term it prohibits national aids to increased production and makes available funds for modernization and rationalization. Other measures include reconversion, research into new product areas and early retirement.

De Gasperi, Alcide (1881 – 1954)
Italian statesman born Trentino and educated in Vienna. Member of the Italian Parliament from 1911, but imprisoned during the Fascist period. After the war he was one of the founders of the Christian Democrat Party and was Prime Minister from 1945 to 1953. During this period he was a strong supporter of moves to link Italy with the countries of Western Europe and ensured Italian membership of the Council of Europe (q.v.) and the North Atlantic Treaty Organization (q.v.). He gave great support to the establishment of the European Coal and Steel Community and suffered disappointment through the failure of the European Defence Community (q.v.). Recipient of the Charlemagne Prize (q.v.) in 1952.

De Gaulle, Charles (1890 – 1970)
French soldier and statesman. Born Lille and graduated from St. Cyr military academy. His career until 1940 was a military one and he rose to the rank of major-general. With the fall of France, de Gaulle crossed to Britain and from there led the 'Free France' movement. After the Liberation he briefly headed the government, but retired in 1946. He was persuaded to emerge from retirement in 1958 following the Algerian crisis and in 1959 became the first President of the Fifth Republic. During his years in office he contributed to the modernization of the country and helped re-establish its self-confidence. He never wavered in his belief that France was a great power and he demonstrated the country's freedom of action by withdrawing from the North Atlantic Treaty Organization (q.v.). At first hostile to the European Community, he was persuaded that it could be an instrument for furthering French interests. To this end he promoted the reconciliation of France with Germany and saw the two countries as central to a united Europe. Great Britain he regarded as a world rather than an European power and he opposed British membership of the Community for fear of the dilution which this could bring about. Under his leadership France was never an easy partner in the E.C., and the crisis of 1965, caused by the disagreement of France with the Commission, caused a weakening of the Community institutions. He was against supranationalism and his ambition was the establishment of the *'Europe des patries.'* His regime was badly shaken by the student revolt in 1968 and he resigned the Presidency in 1969.

De Rougement, Denis
Born Neuchâtel, Switzerland in 1906. Taught at the Universities of Frankfurt, Geneva and New York. A pioneer of modern European unity and in particular of a united states of Europe. Founder and director of the European Cultural Centre at Lausanne. Writer on European and international subjects.

Deniau, Jean François
Former member of the Commission. Born Paris 1928 and graduate of the Ecole Nationale d'Administration. French civil servant involved in the original E.E.C. negotiations and in 1958 appointed Director-General of the Commission's Department of External Relations. Headed the Commission delegation at the enlargement negotiations of 1961 to 1963 and 1969 to 1971. Commissioner from 1967 to 1976 at first with special responsibility for external trade and financial control and subsequently for development aid, cooperation policy, budgets and financial control.

Denmark
Member state of the European Community since 1973. Area of 43 000 km^2 and population of 5.1. millions makes it the smallest member in area except for Luxembourg and in population except for Luxembourg and Ireland. Nevertheless it is one of the more prosperous member states with a relatively high per capital Gross Domestic Product. In modern times this prosperity has been based on a specialist agriculture concentrating on diary and meat products for which the land is well suited. In the early 1950s one quarter of the labour force was still in agriculture, but since then there has been considerable industrial growth particularly in engineering, shipbuilding, chemicals, agricultural machinery, domestic equipment and furniture. As a result 30 per cent of the population is now in industry as compared to 9 per cent in agriculture. Some half of all the country's external trade is with the Community to which Denmark is one of the principal suppliers of foodstuffs. For a long period membership did not appeal to the Danes largely because of the country's traditional ties with her Scandinavian neighbours and also because her largest single export market, the United Kingdom, remained outside. Alongside the United Kingdom and the other Scandinavian countries she became in 1959 a member of the European Free Trade Association (q.v.), but eventually joined the Community at the same time as Britain. There still remains considerable opposition to membership, however. Denmark is a member of most other major western organizations and has remained a member of the Nordic Council (q.v.).

Diane *see* Euronet Diane

Dillon Round
World trade negotiations conducted under the auspices of the General Agreement on Tariffs and Trade (q.v.) and named after the United States negotiator, Douglas Dillon. In 1961 the Commission on behalf of the E.C. signed a general agreement providing for tariff reductions of 20 per cent. *See also* Kennedy Round, Tokyo Round.

Direct elections *see* European Parliament

Directive
A decision taken by Council as the legislative body of the Community. It is similar to a Regulation (q.v.) but is binding only on the governments of the member states.

Dublin
Capital city of the Republic of Ireland and location of the E.C. Irish Office. It is also the headquarters of the European Foundation for the Improvement of Living and Working Conditions (q.v.).

Duisenberg Plan
Plan produced in 1976 by the Dutch Finance Minister, W. F. Duisenberg. It aimed to strengthen the E.C. through a programme of economic and monetary cooperation, and consisted of a package of measures on credit, currency alignment and economic planning. After examination the plan was rejected by the finance ministers of the other members in 1977.

E

East Germany *see* German Democratic Republic

Economic and Monetary Union (E.M.U.)
Policy intention expressed at the Hague Conference (q.v.) in 1969 for the creation of an economic zone with free movement of persons, goods, services and capital. This would constitute an independent monetary whole with fixed parities and complete convertibility. The Werner Plan (q.v.) outlined stages for the achievement of this, and led to closer alignment of economic policies, the introduction of the Snake (q.v.) and the European Monetary System (q.v.).

Economic and Social Committee
Members appointed by the Commission for four year periods from lists submitted by member states. The committee is advisory and must be consulted on questions relating to the free movement of workers, freedom of establishment, freedom of supply services and necessary amendments to national legislation in these fields. The Committee may also act on its own initiative.

Economic Commission for Europe
Established in 1947 by the Economic and Social Council of the United Nations for the purpose of strengthening economic activity in Europe and promoting closer economic relations among the countries of the Continent. Its membership consists of the countries of western and eastern Europe which are members of the United Nations, together with the United States and Canada. It has specialist committees on coal, steel, electricity, transport, manpower and agriculture and issues reports and guidelines. Since 1958 the E.C. Commission has taken part in its activities as a 'guest of the Secretariat.' The headquarters are in Geneva.

Economic Policy Committee
Established by the E.C. in 1974 as a replacement for the Conjunctural Policy, Medium Term Economic Policy and Budgetary Policy Committees. Its task is to oversee and coordinate the economic and financial policies pursued by the Community. It consists of four representatives from each of the member states together with representatives from the Commission.

Economic Zone *see* Exclusive Economic Zone

Edinburgh
Capital city of Scotland and location of the E.C. Scottish Office.

Eggs
There is no system of price control for eggs, but the internal market is protected by import levies. Measures are in force to improve production, quality, processing and sales. Standards are laid down by the Community for grading by quality and weight. Refunds

are available to encourage exports when world prices are higher than prices in the E.C.

Egypt
Middle Eastern state having cooperation agreements with the Community as part of the general agreement with the Mashreq countries (q.v.). Recipient of financial aid and loans from the European Investment Bank (q.v.).

Elections, direct *see* European Parliament

Energy policy
Energy policy at Community level is still in its infancy, most energy matters being still under the control of national governments. Energy was not considered in the treaties as a suitable area for future common action, responsibility for it being dispersed among the three Communites. The European Coal and Steel Community dealt only with coal, and the European Atomic Energy Community was intended specifically to develop nuclear power. All other forms of energy come under the regulatory umbrella of the European Economic Community. This made an overall view of the energy position impossible until the work of the three Communities was integrated. The 1973 Oil Crisis produced a sharp rise in oil prices, and this adversely affected the whole economy. It demonstrated the vulnerability of the Community since 60 per cent of its energy, mostly in the form of oil, had to be imported from overseas. The E.C.'s role since then has largely been to lay down guidelines for action and these were specified in the Saint-Geours report (q.v.). It is regarded as essential to cut consumption through the more rational use of energy, the target for this being one per cent annually. Coupled with this the Commission envisages an increase in Community energy output and a consequent decrease in dependence on external sources of supply. The New Community Instrument (q.v.) makes funds available for the development of alternative energy sources. The nuclear energy field is a specific task of the Joint Research Centre (q.v.). In order to improve security of energy supplies the obligation is imposed on member states to maintain minimum stocks of oil and of fuels for thermal power stations, and energy resources must be shared among members if supplies are interrupted. Since 1973 gross inland consumption of primary energy in the Community has stabilized and dependence on overseas supplies has begun to decrease.

Enlargement of the Community
As specified in the treaties, the E.C. is open to new members so long as they are acceptable unanimously to the existing membership. In 1969 the United Kingdom, Ireland, Denmark and Norway applied for membership and the negotiations were successfully concluded in 1971. Accordingly in 1973 the United Kingdom, Ireland and Denmark became members, but Norway declined to join as the result of an adverse referendum vote. In 1975 Greece applied for membership and following the successful conclusion of negotiations, became a member in 1981. Spain and Portugal applied in 1977 and negotiations were commenced in the following year. Membership negotiations can be both long and difficult, and the applicant has to be seen to be of Community material both economically and politically. Enlargement can also cause economic difficulties for the existing members of the Community.

Environment and Consumer Protection Service
Established by the Commission in 1973 for the purpose of protecting consumers in the E.C. against goods which may be harmful or contain dangerous substances. It also monitors the effects of such products on the environment. The service operates under Community regulations on the quality and safety of products and the provision of compensation for any damage or injury caused.

Environment, Protection of
There is no direct provision in the Treaties for the establishment of a coordinated environmental policy. Consideration of the environment has now become essential as a result of economic growth in the European countries and the development of large urban and industrial complexes. The Environmental Action Programmes established in 1973 aim at the reduction of pollution and nuisances damaging to the environment and to the quality of life. They establish the principle of 'polluter pays' and the need for

preventive action at the most appropriate levels. This is being achieved through regulations, education, information programmes and research into less polluting technologies. Up to 1980 the Community accepted 58 pieces of legislation relating to air pollution, water quality, waste disposal, noise levels and natural resources. It is involved in the protection of birds and their habitats and a scheme for ecological mapping and environmental impact is being assessed. Since environmental pollutants do not stop at national frontiers, the aim is to seek common solutions both within and outside the Community and funds are available for this purpose. There are special programmes for the Rhine (q.v.) and the Mediterranean (q.v.). *See also* Water policy.

Equatorial Guinea
West African state signatory of the Lomé Conventions (q.v.). Former colony of Spanish Guinea which became independent in 1968.

Establishment, right of
One of the rights stipulated in the Treaty of Rome after a transition period. This gives Community nationals and companies the right to establish anywhere in the Community with freedom from any restrictions based on nationality. The only major exception to this is in the field of governmental activities or those closely connected with governments. The right of establishment is closely related to the freedom of movement of workers (q.v.).

Ethiopia
East African state signatory of the Lomé Convention (q.v.). Unlike the other signatories, Ethiopia is not a former European dependency except for Eritrea province, a former Italian colony, with which it federated after the Second World War.

E.U.A.
Abbreviation used for unit of account. *See* European Unit of Account

Euratom *see* European Atomic Energy Community

Euro-Arab Dialogue
This was first mooted in 1973 following the unilateral increase in oil prices by the Organization of Oil Producing Countries (O.P.E.C.). The main dialogue went on between 1975 and 1978 between the Community and the Arab League and took the form of a series of conferences. Little real progress was made on account of the Arab insistence on consideration of the Palestine question, while the Europeans wished to talk primarily about economic matters. There have since been further moves to re-start the Dialogue and in particular to develop a closer relationship with the Gulf States.

Eurocrat
Nickname for bureaucrats in the higher echelons of the service of the Commission.

Eurofer
Cartel of the steel producers in the European Community. It deals with general policy matters and questions of pricing, output, exports and overall development. Discussions take place with the Commission under the provisions of the Treaty of Paris (q.v.). *See also* Davignon Plan.

Euronet Diane
High speed computerized information system established by the Commission and the national postal and telecommunications organizations within the Community. Opened in 1980, it links together all the countries of the Community. The control centre is in London and the other major switching exchanges are Paris, Frankfurt and Rome. Diane (Direct Information Access Network for Europe) is linked to the Euronet telecommunications services and can supply information on a wide range of subjects.

Europa Houses
Institutions established in a number of European countries for the promotion and dissemination of information concerning European affairs. They bring together students, trade unionists, academics and professional groups for the discussion of a wide range of relevant subjects. Their funds come from a number of sources and their activities are coordinated by the International Federation of Europa Houses (F.I.M.E.)

European Agricultural Guidance and Guarantee Fund (E.A.G.G.F.)
Known also by its French initials of F.E.O.G.A. (Fonds Européen d'Orientation et de Garantie Agricole), it was established in 1962 as an instrument of the Common Agricultural Policy (q.v.). It was intended to assist in the modernization of the agricultural sector, to provide secure markets for producers and ensure supplies of agricultural produce to the consumers. The Fund's two main functions are the structural improvement of the agricultural sector and the creation of a system of stable prices. Under the heading of 'guidance,' funds are available to farmers for the improvement of equipment, purchase of materials, reconversion of land, early retirement pensions and special grants for hill farmers (q.v.). Funds used for these purposes make up from 25 to 40 per cent of all such expenditure, the rest being provided by national organizations. The 'guarantee' side is concerned with stabilizing prices and this is done through intervention buying and selling as necessary by Community agencies to keep prices regulated at agreed levels. Storage costs are repaid, refunds made to exporters and subsidies given to certain categories of producers. The E.A.G.G.F. accounts for some two-thirds of all annual expenditure in the Community budget (*see* Budget, Annual Community). By far the largest part of the Fund has been used for price guarantee and only 5 to 6 per cent has normally gone to the guidance section. It has been open to the criticism that it has subsidized inefficiency and overproduction, so producing the 'mountains' and 'lakes,' the disposal of which has presented such problems. At the same time the consumer has had to pay much higher prices than the high levels of production have warranted. In spite of this, the Fund has been a contributary factor in the transformation of European agriculture since the 1950s.

European Assembly *see* European Parliament

European Atomic Energy Community
Familiarly know as 'Euratom,' this organization was one of the two Communities established in 1958 under the Treaties of Rome (q.v.). The emergence of nuclear power as a possible answer to Europe's growing energy deficit and the dangers inherent in its development motivated the establishment of Euratom as a special Community for the purpose of putting it under some form of international control. Four research centres were set up at Karlsruhe (q.v.), Geel (q.v.), Petten (q.v.) and Ispra (q.v.) and it was intended that they should be centres for the coordination of pioneering activity in the field. Achievements were limited by the attitudes of certain member governments increasingly disinclined to accept the internationalization of something of such potential political and economic significance. In 1967 the Euratom Commission was merged with those of the other Communities and the nuclear industry has since been regarded as coming within the Community's overall energy policy (q.v.). Euratom's four establishments are known as the Joint Research Centre (q.v.) which is now mainly concerned with safety measures and environmental impact. It plays a part in the dissemination of information and the coordination of research at national levels and has its own supply agency for fissile materials. Member states are required to inform the Community of all new nuclear investments and Euratom funds are available to assist approved projects.

European Bureau of Consumers Unions (B.E.U.C.)
Established by the national consumer associations in E.C. member countries for the purpose of coordinating their activities at European level. It monitors the E.C.'s consumer programme, especially in the fields of safety, redress and safeguards for shoppers, and gives opinions on appropriate new areas for consumer legislation.

European Centre for the Development of Vocational Training (C.D.E.F.O.P.), *see* Vocational training

European Centre for Nuclear Research (C.E.R.N.)
Established in 1954 for the purpose of coordinating research into the peaceful uses of nuclear energy. Projects undertaken have included sub-nuclear, high-energy and elementary particle physics. The member countries are Austria, Belgium, Denmark, France, the Netherlands, Norway, Sweden, Switzerland and the United Kingdom. There are also a number of observers.

European Coal and Steel Community (E.C.S.C.)
The first of the three Communities. It was based upon the ideas contained in the Schuman Plan (q.v.) and was established by the Treaty of Paris (q.v.) in 1951. It stemmed from the need to find an international solution to the problem of control of Europe's basic industrial resources, and in particular those of Germany. The United Kingdom and many other countries did not see it at the time as being in their interest to join, and the six founder members were France, the Federal Republic of Germany, Italy, the Netherlands, Belgium and Luxembourg. It established a common market in coal, steel, iron, iron ore and scrap and laid down rules for the conduct and the regulation of trade in this market. The E.C.S.C. was controlled by a High Authority of nine members having its headquarters in Luxembourg, its first president being Jean Monnet (q.v.). There was also a Council of Ministers (q.v.) having a supervisory role, a European Court of Justice (q.v.) and a Common Assembly (*see* European Parliament). Following the establishment of this Community there was a great increase in trade among members in the regulated products but, since there was no common external tariff, trade with third countries also increased as the economies grew. The early success of E.C.S.C. led to further ideas for promoting European unity, notable among them being the European Defence Community (q.v.). In 1967 the High Authority was merged with the Commissions of the other two Communities and the headquarters moved to Brussels. It remains a separate juridical entity but its activities are now closely bound up with those of the other Communities.

European Communities (E.C.)
Collective name given to the European Coal and Steel Community (q.v.), the European Economic Community (q.v.) and the European Atomic Energy Community (q.v.). In 1967 the executive bodies were merged and since then there has been a single Commission for all three.

European Communities Act
Act passed by the British Parliament in 1972 giving legal force to the Treaty of Accession (q.v.) signed the previous year. It made all past and future Community legislation binding on the United Kingdom and set up the machinery for the implementation of the regulations on agriculture, international trade and industrial practice.

European Community Youth Orchestra (E.C.Y.O.)
Formed in 1977 of young musicians drawn from all the countries of the European Community. Organized by the International Federation of Youth Orchestras and financed by the Commission, national governments and private enterprise. The orchestra plays at festivals and international musical events throughout Europe.

European company law
The Treaties require mutual recognition of companies, coordination of company law, freedom of establishment and regulations on mergers of companies governed by different national laws. The broad principles have been implemented and legislation has been drafted on the structure of limited companies operating within the E.C., standards for auditing company accounts, information on securities, harmonization of company taxation systems and the control of concentrations. The European company statute (q.v.) is still in preparation.

European company statute
First proposed in 1974 for the purpose of giving companies operating within the Community legal status at Community level. While subject to European company law rather than to national company laws, the taxation system used would be that of the country in which the headquarters were located. European company status would be open to existing companies as well as to new ones, but companies could also retain their national legal status if desired.

European Council
Institutionalization of the periodic summit conferences of Heads of Government which have been taking place since the European Communities were first established. It was resolved at the summit conference of 1974 that as from 1975 the Heads of Government should meet as a Council at least three times a year. It was agreed that there should be regular liaison with the Commission in order to avoid any confusion with the activities of the Council of Ministers (q.v.). The European Council quickly became the major deci-

sion-making body on policy issues leaving the details to be worked out later, Major decisions taken by the Council include the implementation of direct election to the European Parliament, the establishment of the European Monetary System (q.v.) and the modification of the British contribution to the Community budget. This Council is not legally an institution of the Community, but it may take decisions by acting as Council as laid down in the Treaties. All major decisions so taken require unanimity.

European Court of Auditors
Set up in 1975 for the purpose of auditing the accounts of all the Community's constituent bodies and establishing that they are correct and reflect good financial management. The Court is completely independent and the members, who must be specially qualified for their office, are appointed for periods of six years. They are required to draw up an annual report and to give assistance as necessary to the Commission and the European Parliament in framing the budget.

European Court of Justice
Established for the purpose of ensuring the observance of the laws of the Communities as laid down in the Treaties and the appended statutes and regulations. The Court sits in Luxembourg and consists of nine Judges and four Advocates General appointed for six year periods. It is completely independent and the Judges elect their own President. Suits may be filed by member states, Community institutions and private individuals. The Court is the final authority in the interpretation of the laws of the Community and its judgements have immediate effect. Its decisions have been of importance in demonstrating the authority of the Community, interpreting the exact meaning of legislation, and establishing the areas in which Community law now takes precedence over national laws.

European Currency Unit (Ecu)
The currency used in the European Monetary System (q.v.) in place of the European Unit of Account (E.U.A.) (q.v.) with which it is identical in value. Its current value is based on the currencies 'basket' (q.v.) of the member states. On its introduction in 1979 the Ecu was valued at £0.0885.

European Defence Community (E.D.C.)
Following the success of the establishment of the European Coal and Steel Community (q.v.), a further scheme was launched to apply these integrative principles in the area of common defence. This was the Pleven Plan, named after the French Prime Minister of the time, and, like the Schuman Plan before it, it owed much to Jean Monnet (q.v.). It envisaged a common European foreign policy and the setting up of a European army. Although invited to participate, the United Kingdom refused to do so, and the E.D.C. treaty was signed in Paris by the same six countries who had in the previous year established E.C.S.C. The Defence Community never came into existence since, although it was ratified by five of the national parliaments, the French National Assembly refused to do so. The failure of E.D.C. created problems connected with the forthcoming sovereignty of the Federal Republic of Germany (q.v.) but these were resolved in 1955 in the framework of Western European Union (q.v.).

European Democrats (E.D.)
One of the seven party groups in the European Parliament. It has 64 members and consists entirely of the British Conservatives together with Danish Conservatives and one Centre Democrat. All but three of its members are British and the group comes third in size after the Socialists (q.v.) and the European People's Party (q.v.).

European Development Fund
Established for the purpose of providing aid to the dependencies of Community countries and to underdeveloped countries associated with the Community. It has been the major financial instrument of the Yaoundé Conventions (q.v.) and, following that, of the Lomé Conventions (q.v.) and it is also used to aid the Overseas Countries and Territories (q.v.). It provides non-repayable grants, and eligible countries are required to apply for them giving details of the projects to be financed. The Fund's financial participation remains under Community control until the completion of each project. Between 1964 and 1980 4635 million units of account was allocated to over sixty independent countries and dependencies through the European Development Fund.

European Economic Community (E.E.C.)
Set up under the Treaty of Rome (q.v.) in 1957, the E.E.C. came into existence in 1958 with its headquarters in Brussels. Its membership consisted of France, the Federal Republic of Germany, Italy, the Netherlands, Belgium and Luxembourg. It continued the principles of economic cooperation which had been pioneered by the European Coal and Steel Community and extended them to cover the whole range of economic affairs except for nuclear power which was in the hands of its twin, the European Atomic Energy Community (q.v.). A common market was to be created within which there were to be no economic impediments to free trade and policies were to be initiated for dealing with agriculture, transport, social problems, sectoral restructuring and regional development. These were intended to make integration a smoother process and to mitigate difficulties which might otherwise be caused by it. There was also a programme of aid to underdeveloped territories and countries associated with the Community. Full internal free trade was achieved in 1968 and at the same time all restrictions were removed on the freedom of movement of workers (q.v.). Since then the Community has been developing the scope of its policies and has also entered the fields of energy policy, finance, environment and pollution control. The institutions established to run the Community were the Commission, the Council, the European Court of Justice and the European Parliament, the latter three being shared with the other two Communities. In 1967 the Commission was merged with that of the E.A.E.C. and the High Authority of the E.C.S.C., and since then the activities of all three European Communities (E.C.) have been progressively integrated.

European Federalist Movement
This founded in Milan in 1943 as the Movimento Federalista Europea. Its founders were Altiero Spinelli (q.v.), Ernesto Rossi and other members of the Italian resistance to Fascism. Its ideas derived from the Ventotene Manifesto which had outlined a plan for a federal Europe. Its first congress met in Venice in 1946 and the Movement considerably influenced thought on achieving European unity in the post-war years. Following the rejection of the European Defence Community (q.v.) in 1954 its ideas were increasingly seen to be unrealistic, and it ceased to exercise much influence in government circles.

European Foundation for the Improvement of Living and Working Conditions
Established by the E.C. in 1975 with its headquarters in Dublin. It is intended for research into living and working conditions in the Community, and as a clearing house for the exchange of information and experience among member states.

European Free Trade Association (E.F.T.A.)
This was established by the Stockholm Agreements of 1959 and entered into force in 1960. It was a response by the remaining members of the Organization for European Economic Cooperation (q.v.) to the creation of the European Economic Community by six of their number in 1957. These countries wanted a looser grouping than that envisaged in the E.E.C. so that they could maintain greater control over their own economies. They were led in this resolve by the United Kingdom and the other countries involved were Sweden (q.v.), Norway (q.v.), Denmark (q.v.), Switzerland (q.v.), Austria (q.v.) and Portugal (q.v.). In 1956 the O.E.E.C. had established the feasibility of a free trade area in Europe and so the 'Seven' emulated the 'Six' and went ahead with the creation of a grouping which they found acceptable. It consisted of an industrial free trade area with retention of national tariffs against third countries and regulations for origin controls. Trade in agricultural produce was not covered, but there was provision for preferential bi-lateral agreements. E.F.T.A. was subsequently joined by Finland (q.v.) in 1961 and Iceland (q.v.) in 1970 and it achieved full industrial free trade in 1966. The greatest trade increases now took place inside both the 'Six' and the 'Seven' and this tended for a time to polarize Western Europe economically. From the start E.F.T.A. had emphasized close collaboration with the E.E.C., and a number of E.F.T.A. countries envisaged eventual E.E.C. membership. In 1973, following the conclusion of successful negotiations, the United Kingdom and Denmark joined the Community and consequently terminated

their membership of E.F.T.A. The remaining members of the Association then negotiated their own trade agreements with the Community which generally entailed free trade in manufactures and preferential agreements for agricultural products.

European Institutions
Institutions established under the Treaties for the purpose of running the Communities. *See also* Commission, Council of Ministers, European Court of Justice, European Parliament.

European Investment Bank (E.I.B.)
Established under the Treaty of Rome (q.v.) in 1958 for the purpose of contributing to the balanced development of the Community. Its task is to help finance projects in the less developed regions and also projects of particular importance in sectoral and local development. Capital is provided at relatively low rates of interest and assistance is given in projects which might otherwise fail to raise the required funds. Finance is available to public and private projects for up to 50 per cent of their total cost and 'global loans' may also be made to intermediary institutions. The most important recipients have been the peripheral regions, transport undertakings, industrial reconversions, and schemes for development in frontier areas. Large numbers of loans have been made to assist in the building of motorways, pipelines, transmission lines, power stations, steel works, chemical plant and the improvement of railways. The Bank borrows on national and international money markets and loans are guaranteed by the Community governments. Total investment capital now stands at 7200 million European Units of Account (q.v.). Between 1958 and 1973 nearly 60 per cent of all the Bank's loans went to Italy, in particular the Mezzogiorno, and the next largest recipient was France with about a quarter. Since enlargement in 1973 the pattern of loans has somewhat changed and Italy's share has gone down to a third while the United Kingdom's has been over a quarter. The share of France, which comes third, has fallen slightly. Although having the smallest G.D.P., Ireland has had more finance from the Bank than any of the Benelux countries or Denmark. The greater part of the Bank's capital is employed within the Community, but since 1963 it has been available elsewhere. Between 1963 and 1978 loans to the total value of 1320 million E.U.A. were made to Mediterranean countries, in particular Greece, Turkey and Portugal, to the signatories of the Lomé Conventions (q.v.) and to the Overseas Countries and Territories (q.v.). The Bank's activities are controlled by a Board of 17 Directors appointed for five year periods and a Management Committee.

European Launcher Development Organization (E.L.D.O.)
Established for the purpose of promoting joint European space research. Merged with the European Space Research Organization to become the European Space Agency (q.v.). in 1977.

European Monetary Agreement
Replaced the European Payments Union (q.v.) in 1958. It carried on the latter's activities and contributed to the process of economic and monetary cooperation in Western Europe.

European Monetary Cooperation Fund
Established by the E.C. in 1973 for the purpose of managing the Community exchange rate system and the short-term monetary support mechanism. The Fund handles credits made available for currency support measures. It is empowered to intervene if necessary on foreign currency markets and to act as banker to the Community.

European Monetary Fund
It was agreed in 1978 that this would be established within two years as part of the European Monetary System (q.v.).

European Monetary System (E.M.S.)
Established by the Communities in 1979 for the purpose of creating a zone of monetary stability with mutually stable exchange rates. Currencies of the participating countries are to be kept within margins of 2.25 per cent on each side of an agreed central rate and national intervention is required to prevent greater divergence. The European Currency Unit (q.v.) was established for transactions within E.M.S. Member states are required to deposit 20 per cent of their gold and dollar reserves with the European Monetary Cooperation Fund (q.v.) in exchange for which they receive Ecus. Short and medium term financial assistance is available together with loans to less prosperous member states. It was agreed that a European Monetary Fund

would be set up in conjunction with E.M.S. While the United Kingdom is not a participant, the £ Sterling is one of the currencies making up the value of the Ecu.

European Movement
Founded in Paris in 1947 for the purpose of the study and dissemination of information on European unity. It was responsible for convening the Congress of Europe at The Hague in 1948 and has since been active in support of the major organs of European unity. The Movement has national councils in Austria, Belgium, Denmark, France, the Federal Republic of Germany, the Republic of Ireland, Italy, Luxembourg, the Netherlands, Norway, Sweden, Switzerland, Turkey and the United Kingdom.

European Parliament
One of the four principal institutions of the European Communities which had its origins in the Common Assembly of the European Coal and Steel Community. In 1958 this was merged with the Assembly established under the Treaties of Rome (q.v.) and in 1962 it took the official title of European Parliament. It then consisted of 142 members and, following the enlargement of the Community in 1973, this was increased to 198. It was made up of delegates from the national parliaments of member states on an agreed proportional basis, and they were selected by whatever means each member state decided to use. The Treaties gave it no legislative powers and its role was largely a consultative and advisory one. Commissioners were obliged to appear before it to answer questions and to account for their actions, and the Commission could be dismissed 'en bloc' by a two-thirds majority. This considerable power was never used although it was occasionally threatened. As the Community moved towards possession of its own financial resources, Parliament was given certain additional powers, first over the administrative budget and then over the budget as a whole.

In 1979, in accordance with the provisions of the Treaty of Rome, direct elections were held for the European Parliament. It now consists of 434 members, each of the four large countries having 81 members, the Netherlands 25, Belgium and Greece 24, Denmark 16, Ireland 15 and Luxembourg 6. Members sit according to political persuasion and national parties have been merged together into appropriate European groupings. These are, in order of size, the Socialists (q.v.), European People's Party (q.v.), European Democrats (q.v.), Communists (q.v.), Liberal and Democratic Group (q.v.) and Progressive Democrats (q.v.). There is also a group for the Technical Coordination and Defence of Independent Groups and Members. The Parliament is run by a Bureau consisting of a President and twelve Vice-Presidents and in 1979 Simone Veil (q.v.) was elected the first President. Parliament may debate all matters relating to the Community and its policies. Commission proposals are sent to Parliament which delivers its opinion on them. It may amend the budget and these amendments must then be considered by Council. The final budget must be passed by Parliament before it can be implemented. Parliament also retains the power to dismiss the Commission, but in many ways the Commission and Parliament have proved to be allies in pressing new policies upon the Council which is the ultimate legislative organ. Parliament has fifteen committees specializing in such matters as political affairs, transport, external relations, regional policy and budgets and these matters are considered before they reach the floor of the House. Parliament now sees its role as an evolving one and asserts its authority as the only democratically elected institution of the Community. Its secretariat is in Luxembourg, but most of its meetings take place in the *Maison de l'Europe* at Strasbourg. It is widely felt that Parliament should now have a permanent home, and both Luxembourg and Brussels as well as Strasbourg have been proposed for this.

European Patent Convention
Signed in Luxembourg in 1975 by the member states of the European Community, this came into force in 1977. It provides uniform patent protection throughout the Community and supplements the Munich Convention signed in 1973 by sixteen European states. Operation of the Convention is in the hands of the European Patent Office in Munich and there are branches in The Hague and in London.

European Payments Union (E.P.U.)
Established in 1950 by seventeen European states as a clearing house for multilateral debits and credits in their mutual trade. Credit was automatically extended to those

members having balance of payement deficits with other members and was funded by those in surplus. The E.P.U. is regarded as having been an important stimulus to greater economic cooperation in Europe. It was replaced in 1958 by the European Monetary Agreement (q.v.).

European People's Party
One of the seven party groups in the European Parliament. It consists of all the Christian Democrats and the Fine Gael members from Ireland. Its membership is drawn from every Community country except for the United Kingdom and Denmark whose principal right wing parties are non-confessional. Over two-thirds of the members are from Italy and the Federal Republic of Germany. In the direct elections of 1979 it won 107 seats, making it the second largest party group in the European Parliament.

European Political Cooperation
Moves towards establishing closer political cooperation among the members of the European Communities have stemmed from the importance attached to the alignment of policies on matters outside the strict terms of reference of the E.C. Treaties. Such cooperation was developed in the Davignon Committee (q.v.) and is carried on in the work of the Committee of Political Directors (q.v.). The Council of Ministers meets for the discussion of foreign policy issues and when it does so it constitutes a Meeting of Foreign Ministers in Political Cooperation (q.v.).

European Political Community
Proposal arising out of the success of the European Coal and Steel Community and the initial success of the European Defence Community (q.v.) for the setting up of a full political union of the six countries. It was to have a two-chamber legislature, an executive council and a judiciary. The failure of the E.D.C. in 1954 also meant that the idea of a Political Community fell into abeyance.

European Progressive Democrats (D.E.P.)
One of the seven party groups in the European Parliament. It consists mainly of the French Gaullists and the Irish Fianna Fáil, and in the direct elections of 1979 it won 22 seats.

European Recovery Programme *see* Marshall Plan

European Regional Development Fund (E.R.D.F.)
This was established in 1975 and is one of the major instruments of Community regional policy. It is intended to supplement national aids to the poorer regions of the Community and to help frame an overall regional strategy. It was clear that in spite of the great economic advances which had taken place in the Community as a whole, the disparities between richer and poorer regions were still considerable. Positive steps were needed if the situation were to be corrected. The Fund was established with an initial capital of 1300 million units of account (u.a.) for a three year period and was renewed in 1978 for another three year period with a total capital of 2480 million u.a. National shares were agreed upon in advance, the largest being Italy with 40 per cent, the United Kingdom with 27 per cent and France with 17 per cent. Ireland with 6.5 per cent receives more than the Federal Republic of Germany. Regional authorities make applications for aid for specific purposes and the finance is then channelled back through the national governments concerned. Principles insisted upon are those of 'transparency' and 'additionality,' meaning clear use of the resources provided and these being additional to, rather than instead of, national regional aids. While the European Investment Bank (q.v.), the European Agricultural Guidance and Guarantee Fund (q.v.) and the European Coal and Steel Community funds have made an impact on the regional situation, E.R.D.F. is the only one which is specifically designated for regional purposes.

European Research and Development Committee (C.E.R.D.)
Committee set up to advise the Commission on policy in the fields of science and technology.

European Schools
Set up for the purpose of educating the children of staff employed in European institutions in different Community countries. The first was opened in Luxembourg in 1953 to serve the new European Coal and Steel Community established there. Now there are

nine of these schools at Luxembourg, Brussels (2), Varese, Karlsruhe, Munich, Bergen, Mol and Culham. The syllabus is an international one with much attention given to language teaching and the European Baccalaureat provides admission to universities throughout the Community.

European Social Fund
Established in 1960 under the provisions of the Treaty of Rome (q.v.) for the purpose of sustaining and improving the living conditions of workers and their families. At first it supplemented national action in areas of difficulty, notably the older industrial regions and sectors in which there were structural difficulties, but since 1972 the field of its activities has been considerably widened and the finance at its disposal has been increased. The Fund's work is now directed towards a number of priority sectors, these being problem regions, young people, the handicapped, migrant workers, women, adaptation to technological change and agriculture. Training programmes have now been established for workers who have been made redundant by structural and technological change, for those just entering the labour market or wishing to re-enter it, and those in need of special help. Aid has gone to housing and the relocation of families, job creation and allowances for those leaving agriculture, and pilot projects have been undertaken on catering for special needs and problems. It has always been stipulated that all aid provided by the Social Fund must be in addition to, rather than instead of, national social aids.

European Space Agency
Formed by the merger of the European Space Research Organization (q.v.) and the European Launcher Development Organization (q.v.), the aim of the European Space Agency is to develop and apply European space technology. Its headquarters are in Paris and launchings have taken place from the space station at Kourou in French Guiana. Besides all the countries of the European Communities, Spain, Sweden and Switzerland are also members. The immediate programme envisages the launching of satellites to be used for economic and scientific purposes and their development is taking place alongside similar American programmes.

European Space Research Organization (E.S.R.O.)
Merged with the European Launcher Development Organization to become the European Space Agency (q.v.) in 1977.

European Trade Union Confederation (E.T.U.C.)
Established in 1973 by the European affiliates of the International Confederation of Free Trade Unions. Its object was the consideration of matters appropriate to trade unions and in particular those relevant to European conditions. Subsequently other European trade unions, including the Communists, have been accepted for membership.

European Trade Union Institute
Established in 1977 by the Commission and the European Trade Union Confederation (q.v.) and granted a budget by the European Parliament. Its headquarters are in Brussels and its task is to promote better training and information of workers and of their trade union organizations.

European Union
The idea for such a union appeared in the Briand Plan (q.v.) of the inter-war period and emerged again in 1952 as the European Political Community (q.v.). It was revived by the Summit Conference of 1972 which called for 'European union by 1980.' Subsequent reports produced by the Commission and Parliament outlined a structure for such a union including an independent government, an elected parliament sharing in decision-making and a Charter of Civil Rights. In 1975 came the Tindemans Report (q.v.) which further elaborated the possible lines of advance. Although no immediate action followed these reports, such developments as the European Monetary System (q.v.) and direct elections to the European Parliament have been movements in the general direction indicated.

European Unit of Account (E.U.A.)
Adopted by the E.C. in 1974 for the purpose of financing its transactions in the European Investment Bank, the European Development Fund (q.v.) and the European Coal and Steel Community. It was subsequently adopted for the Community budget and for

providing medium-term financial assistance. Its value is based on the 'basket of currencies' (q.v.) of the member states. *See also* European Currency Unit

European University Institute
Established in Florence in 1972 by Community intergovernmental convention to provide facilities for the post-graduate study of European affairs. It was inaugurated in 1976 and offers courses on such subjects as European law, politics and economics.

Eurostat
Name under which the publications of the European Communities Statistical Office in Luxembourg appear.

Excise duty
Tax payable on all products in certain specified categories whether imported or home-produced. The principal duties are on tobacco, wines and spirits and perfume, and they have not been affected by the abolition of general customs duties within the E.C. Their continuance has been objected to on grounds of distortion of trade and discouragement of competition, and a programme leading to eventual harmonization was started in 1974 with the Commission producing a code of principles for their application.

Exclusive dealing agreements
Agreements by which a producer grants the franchise on specific products to a certain distributor within an agreed territory. Such agreements have been held by the European Court of Justice to be in contravention of the Treaty of Rome (q.v.) if they can be proved to be in any way disadvantageous to the consumer. They are acceptable if they can be shown to stimulate trade or help bring about general economic improvement.

Exclusive Economic Zone (E.E.Z.)
The sea area extending from the shores of a coastal state which is deemed to be integral territory for the purposes of resource exploitation. An attempt was made in 1976 by the United Nations Conference on the Law of the Sea to come to an agreement on the permissible extent of such zones and the rights of the riparian states within them. Following the failure of this conference to come to an agreement, the E.C. in 1977 unilaterally declared an exclusive fishing zone of 200 nautical miles around its coasts from which in principle the vessels of third countries are excluded. Similarly the North Sea countries have agreed on zones for the purpose of extracting oil and natural gas from beneath the sea bed. Similar zones have also been demarcated in other parts of the continental shelf around the European coasts. *See also* Common Fisheries Policy.

F

Farm Price Review
Fixing of the common agricultural prices for the following season by Council on the basis of a proposal from the Commission according to the rules laid down under the Common Agricultural Policy (q.v.). The target, guide and norm prices (q.v.) within the Community are in European Units of Account (q.v.).

FAST programme
Programme of forecasting and assessment in the fields of science and technology. Set up in 1979 to investigate the possibilities of long-term scientific developments and to finance and coordinate research and encourage transnational cooperation. Priorities are the development of alternative sources of energy, employment problems and new information technologies. 'Bio-society' is a FAST sub-programme concerned with the uses of bio-technology and its social and economic implications.

Federal Republic of Germany (West Germany)
Founder member state of the European Coal and Steel Community, the European Economic Community and the European Atomic Energy Community (q.v.) and member of most other Western international organizations. Its area of 248 600 km^2 and population of 61.4 millions gives it the highest density of population of any country in the Community apart from those of Benelux. The Federal Republic was created in 1949 out of the British, American and French zones of occupation and is a little over half the size of the German state before the Second World War. The new state became fully sovereign in 1955 and this was coupled with its membership of the North Atlantic Treaty Organization (q.v.) and Western European Union (q.v.). The federal structure was imposed by the former occupying powers and consists of ten länder each possessing considerable authority over internal affairs. Following the defeat and destruction of the Second World War the country recovered rapidly and the 'economic miracle' of the 1950s was achieved using the social market policies advocated by Ludwig Erhardt who was first Minister of Finance and then Chancellor. It now has the strongest economy in the Community and accounts for one third of the total Gross Domestic Product. It is highly interdependent with its E.C. partners and a half of its external trade is conducted with them. Its prosperity is based on its ability to produce a large variety of manufactured goods competitively and to export them successfully both to other Community countries and elsewhere. A dominant theme in West German foreign policy has been close association with its neighbours in Western Europe and this was energetically pursued first by Konrad Adenauer (q.v.) and then by Willy Brandt (q.v.).

F.E.O.G.A. (Fonds Européen d'Orientation et de Garantie Agricole)
see European Agricultural Guidance and Guarantee Fund.

Fiji
Island state in the south Pacific signatory of the Lomé Conventions (q.v.). Former British colony which became independent in 1970 and is now a member of the Commonwealth.

Finet Foundation *see* Paul Finet Foundation

Finland
Neutral north European state which signed an industrial free trade agreement with the E.C. in 1973. This followed the entry into the Community of the United Kingdom, Denmark and Ireland and the subsequent negotiation of trade agreements with the remaining European Free Trade Association (q.v.) countries. Finland became an E.F.T.A. associate in 1961 and is also a member of the Nordic Council (q.v.). Over one-third of Finland's external trade is now with the Community. The country's neutral status made it a suitable location for the Conference on Security and Disarmament in Europe (The Helsinki Conference) in 1975.

Fisheries *see* Common Fisheries Policy

Florence (Firenze)
Location of the European University Institute (q.v.). The city, now the capital of the Italian region of Tuscany, is remarkable for its wealth of artistic and architectural treasures dating from the Renaissance. On the initiative of the Italian government, this was considered to be an appropriate setting for the European University.

Fouchet Committee
Set up by the Community in 1962 under the chairmanship of the French diplomat, Christian Fouchet, in order to work out proposals for moving towards political unity. The proposals proved unacceptable to certain members, in particular the Dutch, and the work of the Committee was terminated inconclusively.

France
Founder member state of the European Coal and Steel Community, the European Economic Community and the European Atomic Energy Community. With an area of 544 000 km^2 France is by far the largest Community country possessing over a third of the total territory. However, in population it comes only third after the Federal Republic of Germany and the United Kingdom, and its population density is under a half that of the two latter countries. Until after the Second World War it was not in the front rank of industrialized states, but since the 1950s, and coinciding with its membership of the Community, it has experienced considerable economic growth and development. Its total Gross Domestic Product is now second in the Community to that of the Federal Republic of Germany. It is the Community's main producer of foodstuffs and metallic ores and has important maufacturing industries. Since the 1950s it has become more economically interdependent with its partners and over a half of its international trade is now conducted with them. While the creation of the Community is inextricably linked with the names of the two Frenchmen Jean Monnet (q.v.) and Robert Schuman (q.v.), France has not always been an easy Community member and has on occasion rejected internationalist solutions to common problems. This was particularly so under the presidency of Charles de Gaulle (q.v.) from 1958 to 1969 during which time a more independent foreign policy was embarked upon and an attempt was made to make the country less dependent on its western allies.

Freedom of Movement of Workers
Freedom of movement within the Community is provided for under the Treaties of Paris and Rome and it was implemented in successive stages in the E.C. (6) until fully achieved in 1968. Under the terms of the Treaties of Accession (q.v.) it was introduced also in the three new member states. Nationals of any one member state are now entitled to reside in the territory of another member for the purpose of working without any restriction being placed on this movement. The only exceptions allowable are those arising from national policy, security or health. Such migrant workers may not in any way be discriminated against in respect of remuneration, conditions of employment, taxation or benefits arising from sickness or unemployment. They may bring with them their dependent relatives and may remain in a country after having obtained specific employment there. Children of such workers have the right to appropriate schooling, including language tuition classes. Work is now prog-

ressing on the mutual recognition of professional qualifications. All this applies only to Community nationals and not to nationals of third countries who are working in the Community.

Fruit and vegetables
Products covered by the Common Agricultural Policy (q.v.). Common Organization of the Market (q.v.) and quality controls are in operation. Imports from third countries are subject to reference price (q.v.). Aid is provided from the European Agricultural Guidance and Guarantee Fund (q.v.) for the production, processing and marketing of citrus fruit, and there are premiums for grubbing up and replacing fruit trees as well as finance for surveys of fruit production potential.

G

Gabon
West African state signatory of the Yaoundé and Lomé Conventions (q.v.). Former French colony which became a fully independent republic in 1960.

Gambia, The
West African state signatory of the Lomé Conventions. Former British colony which became independent in 1965 and is now a republic within the Commonwealth.

Geel
Belgian town in which is located one of the four nuclear research establishments set up by the European Atomic Energy Community (q.v.) and now part of the Joint Research Centre (q.v.).

General Agreement on Tariffs and Trade (G.A.T.T.)
Agreement which came into force in 1948 for the purpose of liberalizing world trade by lowering customs barriers and removing discriminatory measures. By 1980 the agreement had 84 contracting parties. The E.C. is not formally a member of G.A.T.T. but the Commission has been empowered to conduct negotiations on behalf of the Community as a whole. *See also* Dillon Round, Kennedy Round, Tokyo Round.

Generalized System of Preferences (G.S.P.) *see* Lomé Conventions

German Democratic Republic (G.D.R.)
East German Communist state created in 1949 from the Soviet zone of Germany (q.v.). It has under a half the area and one third the population of the Federal Republic of Germany (q.v.) but is the most advanced and prosperous industrial state in Eastern Europe. It is closely associated with the Soviet Union and is a member of the Warsaw Pact and the Council for Mutual Economic Assistance (q.v.). The G.D.R. is not officially recognized by the Federal Republic of Germany but its exports have free entry in consequence of West German insistence that legally there is only one German state.

Germany
Germany was a unified state only between 1871 and 1945. Following defeat in the Second World War it was divided by the victorious powers—the United Kingdom, France, the United States and the Soviet Union—into four zones of occupation. Large territories in the east of the country were at the same time unilaterally detached and added to Poland and the Soviet Union. Increasing discord between the three western powers on the one hand and the Soviet Union on the other eventually led to a division of the country along zonal lines. This was the 'Iron Curtain' which effectively separated the east from the west of the country. The three western zones were fused together in 1949 to form the Federal Republic of Germany (q.v.) and in the same year the Soviet zone became the German Democratic Republic (q.v.). The Federal Republic of

Germany went on to become a member of the European Communities, while the German Democratic Republic joined the eastern bloc's Council for Mutual Economic Assistance (q.v.).

Ghana
West African state signatory of the Lomé Conventions (q.v.). Former British colony of Gold Coast, together with the mandated British territory of Togo. It attained independence in 1957 and is now a republic within the Commonwealth.

Giolitti, Antonio
Member of the Commission. Born Rome 1915 and educated at the University of Rome. Active in the Resistance during the Second World War and subsequently a member of the Italian Communist party. In 1958 joined the Socialist party and during the 1960s and 1970s was Minister for the Budget and Economic Planning in three centre-left governments. Became a member of the Commission in 1977 with responsibility for coordination of Community funds and regional policy. Author of works on European left wing politics.

Golden Triangle, The
Triangular area with apexes in the West Midlands, the Ruhr and Paris. A concept introduced by economic geographers in the 1960s to delimit the most advanced and prosperous areas in Western Europe and those which consequently were considered to have the greatest prospects for growth in the new conditions being created by the E.C. *See also* Heavy Industrial Triangle.

Great Britain *see* United Kingdom

Greece
Member state of the European Community since 1981. It is a relatively small country with a total area of 132000 km^2 and a population of 9.3 millions. Its total GDP is less than that of any other member except for Ireland and Luxembourg, and it has in general a less developed economy. This can be seen from the fact that 28 per cent of the labour force is in agriculture and only 30 per cent in industry, while the comparable average figures for E.C. (9) are 8.2 per cent and 40 per cent. Following the defeat of the Communists in the Civil War (1946–1949) Greece became a democratic monarchy, but this situation was brought to an end by the military *coup d'état* in 1967. This inaugurated the 'Greek Colonels' regime which lasted until 1974 when democratic government was restored. Since 1975 the country has been a democratic 'Hellenic Republic.' For most of the time since the Second World War Greek foreign policy has been motivated by the desire for closer relations with the western countries. Greece became a member of the North Atlantic Treaty Organization (q.v.) in 1952 and an associate member of the E.C. in 1962. This entitled her to Community aids and to preferential trade arrangements. The association was frozen by the E.C. during the military regime, but negotiations for full membership were resumed by the Karamanlis government in 1975 and were successfully concluded in 1978. Around 45 per cent of all the country's external trade is now intra-Community, and Greece is an important exporter of Mediterranean agricultural products to the other members.

'Green' currencies *see* Monetary compensatory amounts

'Green Pool'
Name given to the evolving agricultural policy of the E.C. during the 1960s. *See also* Common Agricultural Policy.

Greenland
Large island in the Arctic Ocean which has been part of the European Community since 1973 by virtue of the fact that it is a Danish dependency. It has internal self-government and also sends representatives to the Danish Folketing. Its total area of 2.18 million km^2 makes it considerably larger than the whole of the rest of the Community, but its total population is only 50 000. Most of these live in the far south which is the only really inhabitable part for Europeans.

Grenada
Small island state in the Caribbean signatory of the Lomé Conventions (q.v.). Former British colony which became independent in 1974 and is now a member of the Commonwealth.

Grundig – Consten agreement
Sales agreement made between the German Grundig company and the French Consten

company. It was declared invalid by the Commission in 1964 as being in contravention of the rules prohibiting agreements which prevented or distorted competition. This decision was challenged by Consten which cited Article 85 of the Treaty of Rome permitting such agreements if they contributed to an improvement in production or distribution. The Court ruled in favour of the Commission and the agreement was declared illegal.

Guide price
Price which the producer of certain agricultural products is guaranteed under the Common Agricultural Policy (q.v.). The products covered are beef, veal and wine. *See also* Target price.

Guinea
West African state signatory of the Lomé Conventions (q.v.). Former French colony which became a fully independent republic in 1958.

Guinea-Bissau
Small West African state signatory of the Lomé Conventions (q.v.). Formerly Portuguese Guinea which became an independent republic in 1974.

Gulf States
Riparian states of the Persian Gulf including Iran, Iraq, Kuwait, Saudi Arabia, Bahrain, Quatar and Oman. This is the world's most important oil producing and exporting region and of crucial importance as a supplier to the E.C. *See also* Euro–Arab Dialogue

Gundelach, Finn Olav (1925 – 1981)
Former member of the Commission. Born Vejle, Denmark. Educated University of Aarhus and entered Danish diplomatic service. Rose to become permanent representative of Denmark at the United Nations in Geneva and a Director and Deputy Director-General of the General Agreement on Tariffs and Trade (q.v.). Head of the Danish mission to the European Communities from 1967 to 1972. Commissioner from 1973 to 1981 first with responsibility for internal market and the administration of the customs union and, after 1977, for agriculture and fisheries. Died shortly after appointment as Commissioner for the third time and replaced by Poul Dalsager (q.v.).

Guyana
South American state signatory of the Lomé Conventions (q.v.). Formerly the colony of British Guiana, it became independent in 1966 and is now a republic within the Commonwealth.

Haferkamp, Wilhelm
German member of the Commission. Born Duisburg in 1923 and educated at Cologne University. From 1950 to 1967 employed by the German Trade Union Confederation first as Head of the Social Policy Department in the regional centre of Nordrhein-Westfalen and subsequently as centre president. After 1962 he was head of the Confederation's Federal Economic Policy Department. A member of the Landtag of Nordrhein-Westfalen from 1958 to 1967. Appointed Commissioner in 1967, first with responsibility for energy, then for economic and monetary affairs and since 1977 for external relations. A Vice-President of the Commission since 1970.

Hague Conference
Summit meeting of the heads of state of the E.C. (6) held in 1969. The initiatives taken there produced the *'relance'* (q.v.) of the Community after a period of stagnation. There was a move towards achieving economic and monetary union, reform of the Social Fund and enlargement to include the United Kingdom and other countries.

Hague Congress
Organized in 1948 by the International Committee of the Movements for European Unity and attended by a large number of eminent people from all over the Continent. Means to achieve closer unity among the European countries were discussed and pressure subsequently exerted on governments led to the establishment of the Council of Europe (q.v.).

Hallstein, Walter
First President of the Commission. Born 1901 in Mainz and educated at the Universities of Bonn, Munich and Berlin. Became Professor at the Universities of Berlin, Rostock and Frankfurt. Leader of the German delegation to the Schuman Plan (q.v.) conference in 1950. Secretary of State for Foreign Affairs in the Federal cabinet from 1951 to 1958, during which time he was author of the 'Hallstein Doctrine' on non-recognition of communist regimes in Eastern Europe. President of the Commission from 1958 to 1967 during which time he steered the Community through its early years and established the central role of the Commission in the Community's affairs. From 1968 to 1974 he was President of the European Movement (q.v.) and was a member of the Bundestag from 1969 to 1972. Recipient of the Charlemagne Prize (q.v.) in 1961.

Harmonization
It is the aim to achieve standardization of national legislation in a number of fields throughout the Community so as to promote full and unfettered competition and to maximize the advantages from trade. Harmonization affects tax laws and excise duties, production and marketing of agricultural products and legislation regarding disease in plants and animals. *See also* Value Added Tax.

Health Services, reciprocal benefits
Nationals of Community countries when visiting other Community countries for business or pleasure have the same rights to

medical treatment as have nationals of the host country themselves. The charge for such treatment is refundable by the health services of the recipient's home country.

Heath, Edward
Former British Prime Minister. Born 1916 in Broadstairs, Kent. Educated Oxford University and entered politics as a Conservative M.P. in 1950. From the beginning an enthusiastic supporter of British participation in the movement towards European unity, he was minister in charge of the first negotiations for British membership of the E.C. from 1961 to 1963. These achieved considerable early success, but failed largely owing to the reluctance of President de Gaulle (q.v.) to accept the United Kingdom as a member. Heath was Prime Minister from 1970 to 1974 and energetically pursued the new negotiations for British membership. These were successfully concluded and the United Kingdom became a member in 1973. He was subsequently an ardent champion of British membership at a time when there was considerable opposition to it from many quarters. Recipient of the Charlemagne Prize (q.v.) in 1963.

Heavy Industrial Triangle
Area enclosed within the triangle stretching across the internal E.C. frontiers from South Belgium to the Ruhr and Lorraine. Within it is located the greater part of the coal production and a substantial part of the iron and steel capacity of the countries of the original European Coal and Steel Community. The control of these important resources played an important part in European politics in the first half of the twentieth century. The European Coal and Steel Community was an attempt to resolve the problem of control of this area and to establish peace and economic unity there. *See also* Golden Triangle.

High Level Steering Group
Committee of senior officials from member states meeting to concert general economic policies and deal with immediate issues in as flexible a way as possible. It is serviced by the Council secretariat and meets as often as required.

Hill farming
A directive (q.v.) of 1975 set out the conditions for grants of special aid to maintain agricultural activity in those areas of the Community in which, as a result of adverse physical conditions, policies implemented by the European Agricultural Guidance and Guarantee Fund (q.v.) are unable to ensure adequate incomes to the farmers. Such areas include much of highland Britain, western Ireland, the Massif Central in France and mountainous regions in Italy. These cover a quarter of the Community's farmland, but account for only 10 per cent of its agricultural production. Annual compensatory allowances are given to farmers in these areas who undertake to continue in farming for a stipulated period of time.

Hillery, Patrick John
President of the Republic of Ireland and former member of the Commission. Born 1923 in County Clare and educated University College, Dublin. Entered politics in 1951 as a member of the Fianna Fáil party and subsequently served as Minister of Education. Commerce and Industry, and Labour. In 1969 he was appointed Minister for Foreign Affairs and in this capacity he successfully negotiated his country's membership of the Community. Following Irish entry in 1973 he became Commissioner in charge of social policy and also a Vice-President. He was elected President of the Irish Republic in 1976.

Hinterscheid, Mathias
General Secretary of the European Trade Union Confederation (q.v.). Born Dudelange, Luxembourg in 1931. Metalworker in the ARBED works who rose to become General Secretary of the Luxembourg Confédération Générale du Travail and subsequently President of the Luxembourg Workers Union. General Secretary of E.T.U.C. since 1976.

Holland
Holland is the richest and most important of the historic provinces of the Netherlands and still dominates the country's commerce and industry. It is now divided for administrative purposes into two provinces, North and South Holland, and they have a combined population of 5.4 millions. This is 40 per cent of the country's population on 14 per cent of its territory. Together the provinces contain the greater part of the conurbation of Randstad which includes the major cities of Amsterdam, Rotterdam and the Hague.

Hong Kong
British Crown Colony in the Far East. Exporter of a diversity of manufactured goods to the E.C. and especially to the United Kingdom. In 1974 it concluded a bilateral voluntary restraint agreement on the export of textile goods to the E.C. under the Multi-fibre Agreements (q.v.).

I

Iceland

Small island state in the North Atlantic which entered into a preferential trade agreement with the E.C. in 1973. This followed the enlargement of the Community and the subsequent negotiation of trade agreements with the remaining members of the European Free Trade Association (q.v.) of which Iceland is a member. Barriers to free trade are to be lowered over a stipulated period, but certain restrictions remain including the export levy on fish products. Iceland is a member of the North Atlantic Treaty Organization (q.v.) and the Nordic Council (q.v.).

Immigration *see* Freedom of movement of workers

India

Commonwealth state which signed a non-preferential commercial cooperation agreement with the E.C. following British membership in 1973. Special agreements safeguard Indian exports to the Community of cane sugar, coir, jute and textile products.

Industrial policy

Many sectors of Community industry have in recent years been facing problems as a consequence of a variety of adverse conditions. These include the rise in energy costs, low levels of capital investment and competition from newer industries in third countries. The achievement of the common market in manufactured goods has also had adverse effects on certain industries in some countries. The Community has been active in attempting to alleviate these problems and has aided industrial restructuring particularly in the fields of coal mining, steel manufacture, textiles, shipbuilding and footwear. Action has included aid to affected industries, attempts to create new jobs and negotiations with third countries to curb imports. On the other side of the coin there has also been aid to assist the development of growth industries, notably aerospace, data processing and electronics, pharmaceuticals and the exploitation of alternative energy sources.

Institutions of the European Communities

The institutions were established under the Treaties, but they have since been added to, and in many cases their functions have been modified. *See also* Commission; Committee of Permanent Representatives; Council of Ministers; High Authority; European Council; European Court of Justice; European Parliament.

Intervention price

Price determined under the Common Agricultural Policy (q.v.) at which the intervention agencies are obliged to buy products offered to them. The products covered are cereals, sugar, butter, powdered milk, certain cheeses, olive oil, colza, sunflower seed, beef and veal, pigmeat and tobacco.

Iran

Middle Eastern state having non-preferential agreement with the E.C. on trade in certain hand-made textile products.

Ireland, Republic of

Member state of the European Community since 1973. Area 70 000 km^2 and population 3.2 millions, giving an overall density of 45 per km^2 which is the lowest in the Community. The modern state dates from 1922 when Ireland was partitioned after a long period of conflict with the United Kingdom dating back to the previous century. The 'twenty-six counties' of the south separated from the United Kingdom of which they had until then been an integral part, while the 'six counties' of the north remained within the United Kingdom. At first the new country had dominion status as the Irish Free State and later as Eire, but in 1949 it left the Commonwealth and assumed the title of the Republic of Ireland. Although it is fifth in size among Community members, with 4.6 per cent of the total area, it has only 1 per cent of the Community's population and 0.6 per cent of its Gross Domestic Product. It remains basically a rural country and a quarter of the employed population is still in agriculture. Following independence its economic links with the United Kingdom remained very close, and part of the attraction of Community membership was the hope of diversifying its external trade. Some 73 per cent of imports and 78 per cent of exports are now with the Community, the highest proportions of any member state. Agricultural products make up 40 per cent of the country's exports, a much larger proportion than that of any other Community member, and it is an importer of manufactured goods. Much of the country is by West European standards underdeveloped and considerable Community aid has been made available, particularly to the western areas. The question of Northern Ireland (q.v.) and its relationship with the Republic has remained a continuing source of friction with the United Kingdom.

Ispra

Town in Northern Italy which is the location of one of the four nuclear research establishments set up by the European Atomic Energy Community (q.v.) and now part of the Joint Research Centre (q.v.).

Israel

Eastern Mediterranean state having industrial free trade and economic cooperation agreements with the Community. It is a recipient of loans from the European Investment Bank (q.v.) and E.C. tariff preference is given on its exports of agricultural goods.

Italy

Founder member state of the European Coal and Steel Community, the European Economic Community and the European Atomic Energy Community. With an area of 300 000 km^2, it comes second to France in size and its population of 56.5 millions makes it one of the more populous of the member states. In spite of the efforts of the Fascist regime in the inter-war period, Italy remained a relatively underdeveloped country until after the Second World War. There was then a complete break with the economic and political nationalism of the immediate past, and the country entered vigorously into the movement for greater European unity. The growth associated with the 'economic miracle' of the 1950s produced a transformation of the country and set it on course to become an economic heavyweight. It is now a major producer and exporter of manufactured goods, in particular electrical and domestic equipment, motor vehicles and synthetic materials. It also exports Mediterranean agricultural products such as citrus fruits, vegetables and wines. Its economic interdependence with the other members of the Community has increased, and nearly a half of its total foreign trade is now conducted with them. The main centre of the country's economic strength is in the north, while the 'Mezzogiorno' south of Rome is a problem area which has been a major recipient of Community aid since the 1950s. Italy is a member of most western international organizations and has been a participant in the world economic summits held since 1978.

Ivory Coast (Côte d'Ivoire)

West African state signatory of the Yaoundé and Lomé Conventions (q.v.). Former French colony which became fully independent in 1960.

J

Jamaica

Caribbean state signatory of the Lomé Conventions (q.v.). Former British colony which became independent in 1962 and is now a member of the Commonwealth.

Japan

One of the major economic powers in the world and an important trading partner of the Community. It exports large quantities of manufactured goods to the Community, in particular motor vehicles and electrical and electronic equipment, and has been running a considerable trade surplus over the years. Currently it provides 2.4 per cent of total Community imports, but takes only 1 per cent of exports. Its penetration of Community markets has been aided by the tariff reductions negotiated under the auspices of the General Agreement on Tariffs and Trade (q.v.). Attempts have been made by the Commission and by the individual governments to redress the balance by increasing Community exports to Japan and at the same time stabilizing imports. The easy penetration of European markets by the Japanese has been a contributory cause of the difficulties faced by many Community manufacturing industries.

Jenkins, Roy

Former President of the Commission. Born Cardiff, Wales in 1920 and educated at the University of Oxford. After war service entered politics in 1948 as Labour Member of Parliament for Southwark, and held office as Parliamentary Private Secretary to the Secretary of State for Commonwealth Relations. From 1950 to 1976 he was Member of Parliament for the Stechford constituency of Birmingham. In the Labour government of 1964 he held office successively as Minister of Aviation, Home Secretary and Chancellor of the Exchequer, and he again held office as Home Secretary in the Labour government of 1974. A strong supporter of British participation in the movement for European unity and of British membership of the E.C. President of the Commission from 1977 to 1981, during which period there were a number of important developments. These included consolidation of the Regional Fund, the establishment of the European Monetary System (q.v.), the extension of Community action in such fields as energy and environmental policy and the enlargement of the Community to include Greece (q.v.). The right of the President to represent the Community at international gatherings was also recognized. However, the Commission had to accommodate itself to institutional changes notably the emerging role of the European Council (q.v.) and of the directly elected European Parliament. Roy Jenkins is President of the United Kingdom Council of the European Movement (q.v.) and of the Labour Committee for Europe, and is the author of a number of political biographies and of books on democratic socialism. He was awarded the Charlemagne Prize (q.v.) in 1972.

Joint European Torus (J.E.T.)

A Community project for the production of economically viable energy supplies using the process of nuclear fusion. It was established with Community funds in 1979 at Culham, Oxfordshire. The Torus itself is an electromagnetic ring within which very high temperatures are produced and nuclear energy released. The aim is the eventual construction of a full-sized thermo-nuclear fusion reactor. Torus is the largest such nuclear fusion project in the world.

Joint Research Centre (J.R.C.)
The collective name for the Community's four nuclear research establishments located at Ispra (Italy), Karlsruhe (Federal Republic of Germany), Geel (Belgium) and Petten (Netherlands), which were originally set up in 1958 under the auspices of the European Atomic Energy Community. Their principal activities are now in the fields of nuclear safety and environmental protection, notably the disposal and storage of nuclear waste, atmospheric pollution and the protection of the seas. An important activity and one pioneered at Ispra, is the 'Super-Sara' project on the behaviour of reactor fuel in the case of a loss of coolant such as occurred in 1979 at the Three Mile Island power station in the U.S.A.

Jordan
Middle Eastern state having cooperation agreements with the Community as part of the general agreement with the Mashreq countries (q.v.). Jordan receives financial aid and loans from the European Investment Bank.

K

Karlsruhe

West German city which is the location of one of the four nuclear research establishments set up by the European Atomic Energy Community (q.v.), now part of the Joint Research Centre (q.v.).

Kennedy Round

World trade negotiations conducted by 49 countries under the auspices of the General Agreement on Tariffs and Trade (q.v.) between 1964 and 1967 and named after the late American President John F. Kennedy. Their aim was to reduce trade barriers and so stimulate world trade, and they concluded with the Geneva Protocol listing tariff concessions which averaged between 35 and 40 per cent. The E.C. is not formally a member of G.A.T.T., but the Commission was empowered to conduct negotiations on behalf of the Community as a whole. The tariff reductions agreed to by the Community were implemented in two stages, two-fifths in 1968 and the remainder in 1970.

Kenya

East African state signatory of the Arusha and the Lomé Conventions (q.v.). Former British colony which became independent in 1963 and is now a republic within the Commonwealth.

Kiribati

Pacific island state signatory of the Lomé Conventions (q.v.). Formerly part of the British protectorate of the Gilbert and Ellice Islands, it became independent in 1980 and is now a member of the Commonwealth.

Kirk, Sir Peter (1928 – 1977)

British and European political leader. Educated at the Universities of Oxford and Zurich. Entered politics as Conservative M.P. for Gravesend in 1955 and, following British membership of the E.C. in 1973, became leader of the Conservative group in the European Parliament. Promoted the idea of a strong role for Parliament in Community affairs. Knighted in 1976.

Kok, Wim

President of the European Trades Union Confederation (q.v.). Born Bergambacht, South Holland in 1938. Entered trade union affairs in 1959 in the building union and rose to the executive of the Netherlands Federation of Trade Unions. Member of the executive of the E.T.U.C. in 1973 and President in 1979.

Kontogeorgis, George

Member of the Commission. Born Tinos 1912 and educated at the University of Athens and in the United States. Official in the Ministry of Commerce, becoming Director-General for Trade until 1967 when he was dismissed by the military dictatorship. In 1973 became Secretary-General for Tourism and then Secretary of State for Coordination and Planning. In 1977 elected to Parliament as a member of the New Democracy Party and appointed Minister in charge of relations with the European Communities. In this capacity he directed the negotiations which led to Greek membership of the E.C. Appointed Commissioner in 1981 with special responsibility for transport policy and fisheries.

L

Lamb *see* Mutton and lamb

'Lamb War'
The dispute between France and the United Kingdom in 1979–1980 which arose out of French fears of the effects of unrestricted British lamb imports on their own producers. Since lamb was not at the time a product covered by the common organization of the market, the French unilaterally restricted these imports. Since then market regulation under the Common Agricultural Policy (q.v.) has been in operation. *See also* Mutton and lamb.

Lardinois, Petrus Josephus
Former Dutch member of the Commission. Born Noorbeek, Limburg in 1924 and educated Wageningen Agricultural University. From 1951 employed by the Dutch government as agricultural advisory officer. Entered politics in 1964 as a member of the Upper Chamber of the States-General, and subsequently held the post of Minister of Agriculture and Fisheries. Member of the Commission from 1973 to 1977 in charge of agricultural matters.

Latin America, relations with
The European Community maintains relations with a number of regional economic groupings in Latin America. These include the Latin American Free Trade Association (L.A.F.T.A.), the Caribbean Community (CARICOM), the Economic Committee for Latin America (C.E.P.A.L.), the Andean Group (q.v.) and the Latin American Economic System (S.E.L.A.). This latter was established in 1975 for the purpose of coordinating the policies of existing groups and giving a new impetus to regional economic cooperation. The countries of the region are now recipients of Community financial and technical aid and joint groups of experts meet regularly to examine particular problems. E.C.–Latin American Interparliamentary Conferences have taken place periodically since 1974 and discussion has taken place on a wide range of matters of common interest.

Lebanon
Eastern Mediterranean state having cooperation agreements with the Community as part of the general agreement with the Mashreq countries (q.v.). A recipient of loans from the European Investment Bank (q.v.).

Lesotho
Small state in southern Africa signatory of the Lomé Conventions (q.v.). Former British colony which attained independence in 1966 and is now a member of the Commonwealth.

Levy *see* Common External Levy

Liberal and Democratic Group
One of the seven party groups in the European Parliament. It has 40 members drawn from all the countries of the Community

except for the United Kingdom which, as a consequence of the system chosen for the direct elections of 1979, has no Liberal members. This group comes fifth in size in the Parliament.

Liberia
West African state signatory of the Lomé Conventions (q.v.). Established in 1822 by the American Colonization Society as a home for freed slaves, it has always maintained close relations with the United States.

Lomé
Capital of the Republic of Togo (q.v.). Location of the signing of the Lomé Conventions.

Lomé Conventions
The first Lomé Convention was signed in 1975 and it replaced the Yaoundé Conventions (q.v.) between the Community and the associated overseas states. Lomé I covered the period 1976 to 1980 and in 1979 it was renewed, Lomé II covering the period from 1980 to 1985. There were 46 signatories to the first Convention, but by 1980 the number of participants had grown to 60. Almost all these African-Caribbean-Pacific (A.C.P.) countries are ex-colonies of European powers, the number of these having been augmented considerably when the United Kingdom became a member of the Community in 1973. The overwhelming proportion of the A.C.P. group, in numbers, population and territory are either African or islands of the African coasts. The provisions of the two Conventions are very similar. The A.C.P. countries have duty-free access for almost all their products into the Community except for those which come under the marketing arrangements of the Common Agricultural Policy, although these latter do have preferential treatment. Special provisions are laid down for those products which are of special importance in the economies of certain A.C.P. countries and these include sugar (q.v.), bananas, rum, beef and veal, and tomatoes. The E.C. guarantees continuity of the market for these products. The Community does not insist in return on the granting of reciprocal preferences, although 'most favoured nation' treatment must apply to Community exports and there must be no discrimination among the E.C. states. Within these provisions the exact tariff arrangements are a matter for bi-lateral agreement between each individual signatory and the E.C. Another important feature is the mechanism for the stabilization of earnings from raw material exports by the A.C.P. countries. This STABEX system (q.v.) is designed to insure exports against any shortfall in earnings resulting either from production difficulties due to natural causes or from changes in the overall economic situation. Compensation can be provided up to an agreed level over a wide range of products, these being mostly tropical plantation crops and certain minerals. Under Lomé I the total aid provided by the Community to the A.C.P. countries was 3390 million units of account (q.v.), and 3000 million of this was from the European Development Fund (q.v.), the greater part of it being made up of grants. Some 375 million u.a. was set aside for the implementation of STABEX. another 390 million u.a. was in the form of loans from the European Investment Bank (q.v.). Aid has been provided for a very large number of projects throughout the A.C.P. countries, particularly for land improvement, marketing, education and technical training, raw material extraction and the construction of infrastructures such as roads and railways. It is up to each individual country to submit projects for consideration and the E.D.F. is the agency not only for financing them but for ensuring that they are carried out as planned. The total sum allocated under Lomé II is 5600 million E.U.A. (q.v.) and the basic conditions are the same as for the previous allocation. However,the aid is being particularly directed towards the poorest among the A.C.P. countries, and there is special emphasis on rural development and on the financing of projects involving more than one country. A sum is also set aside for relief of natural disasters. Nationals of A.C.P. states working in the Community are guaranteed the same rights in all ways as Community nationals and this is reciprocated by the A.C.P. countries themselves. The overall authority for the working of the Convention is the Joint A.C.P./E.C. Council of Ministers, and under this comes the Committee of Ambassadors. There is also a Consultative Assembly which considers the progress of the Convention, a committee on industrial cooperation and the Centre for Industrial Development located in Brussels which has the task of implementing the programme of industrial cooperation.

Luns, Joseph
Born Rotterdam 1911. Dutch politician and active supporter of European cooperation. As Minister of Foreign Affairs between 1956 and 1971 he was a signatory of the Treaty of Rome and subsequently a member of the Council of Ministers. Former President of the Council of the North Atlantic Treaty Organization and Chairman of the Organization for Economic Cooperation and Development (q.v.). Since 1971 Secretary-General of N.A.T.O. Awarded the Charlemagne Prize (q.v.) in 1967.

Luxembourg, Grand Duchy of
Founder member state of the European Coal and Steel Community, the European Economic Community and the European Atomic Energy Community (q.v.), and a location of their institutions. With an area of 2600 km^2 and population of 355 000, Luxembourg is by far the smallest of the Community's members. It maintained its independence as a result of a number of historical factors and remained outside the German Empire in 1871. After the First World War, recognizing that total independence was unrealistic, it negotiated the Belgo-Luxembourg Economic Union (q.v.) which came into existence in 1922. This has subsequently been basic to the country's economic life, and it was followed after the Second World War by the Benelux Union (q.v.). The native language is the old Germanic dialect of Letzeburgesch, but French is now the official language and German is widely spoken. In 1952 Luxembourg's capital city became the headquarters of the new European Coal and Steel Community, as a consequence both of Luxembourg's neutral position in Western Europe and the importance of the country's iron and steel industry. After the integration of the Communities in 1968, E.C.S.C. headquarters moved to Brussels and Luxembourg is now the home of the Court of Justice (q.v.), the European Investment Bank (q.v.) and the secretariat of the European Parliament. It is also one of the meeting places of the Parliament and in 1980 a large new assembly hall was completed for this purpose. The iron and steel industries remain very important and the country's economy is now closely linked to neighbouring regions, especially Lorraine to the south.

Luxembourg, City of
Capital of the Grand Duchy of Luxembourg, with a population of 77 000. Luxembourg has through much of its history been a fortress city and this helped ensure its independence. It is now the home of many of the institutions of the European Community which are located on the Kirchberg plateau to the north of the city.

Luxembourg Agreement
Resolution of a major Community crisis which took place between June 1965 and February 1966. It followed the submission by the Commission to the Council of Ministers of a package of proposals concerning the direct financing of the Common Agricultural Policy (q.v.) from the Community's own revenues. Coupled with this it proposed an increase in the powers of the European Parliament over the budget. These proposals proved unacceptable to the French government and in the absence of any resolution of the problem the French withdrew from participation in the Community's affairs leaving an 'empty chair.' To them the issue was also bound up with majority voting in the Council of Ministers which, under the treaty, was to enter into force in January 1966. After much negotiation, a compromise solution was reached by the Council in Luxembourg in February 1966, and this enabled the French to resume participation. The substance of the agreement was that unanimity would continue to be required in matters where any member state felt its 'vital interests' were likely to be affected. It was also laid down that the Commission should in future consult with member governments before submitting proposals to the Council of Ministers, and the powers of the Commission to deal with third countries on behalf of the Community were subjected to certain restrictions.

M

Macao

Portuguese overseas territory in the Far East, signatory of a bilateral voluntary restraint agreement on the exports of textile products to the E.C. under the Multifibre Agreements (q.v.).

Madagascar

Island state off the eastern coast of Africa signatory of the Yaoundé and Lomé Conventions (q.v.). Former French colony which became independent in 1960.

Maghreb countries

The three north African countries of Algeria (q.v.), Morocco (q.v.) and Tunisia (q.v.). Collective signatories of cooperation agreements with the E.C. in the fields of trade, economic policy, finance, aid and social matters. Recipients of loans from the European Investment Bank (q.v.) to finance projects in the fields of production, infrastructure and training programmes. There is freedom of access for Maghreb exports to the E.C. except for those products covered by the Common Agricultural Policy (q.v.) for which there are tariff preferences. In return a minimum of 'most-favoured-nation' treatment is granted on Community exports. Reciprocal concessions are in operation relating to pensions and social security benefits for E.C. and Maghreb nationals working in one another's countries. A Cooperation Council has been established to oversee the agreement and to promote institutional contacts. The agreements with Maghreb are a part of the Community's overall Mediterranean Policy (q.v.).

Malagasy Republic *see* Madagascar

Malawi

State in southern Africa signatory of the Lomé Conventions (q.v.). Formerly the British protectorate of Nyasaland, the country became independent in 1964 and is now a republic within the Commonwealth.

Malaysia

Commonwealth state in the Far East. Signatory of a bilateral voluntary restraint agreement on the export of textile products to the E.C. under the Multifibre Agreements (q.v.).

Malfatti, Franco Maria

Former President of the Commission. Born Rome 1927. Entered politics as a Christian Democrat in 1958. Held office as Under-Secretary for Foreign Affairs, Minister for State Industries and Minister for Posts and Telegraphs. President of the Commission from 1970 to 1972. He resigned unexpectedly before the end of his term and returned to Italian politics.

Mali

West African state signatory of the Yaoundé and Lomé Conventions (q.v.). Former French colony of Soudan which became independent in 1960.

Malta

Mediterranean island state and member of the Commonwealth. Signatory of an association agreement with the Community. This provides for the progressive elimination of trade barriers in most areas and for preferential access on a reciprocal basis in the remainder. There is also a provision for industrial and technical cooperation and for financial aid to Malta in the form of loans from the European Investment Bank (q.v.) and some grants.

Mansholt, Dr Sicco

Former member and President of the Commission. Born Ulrum, Groningen, in 1908. Tea planter and later farmer who entered politics as a Socialist in 1937. After wartime activity with the Dutch resistance he became Minister of Agriculture in a number of post-war governments. Appointed Vice-President of the Commission in 1958 with special responsibility for agriculture, and was the principal architect of the Common Agricultural Policy (q.v.). The Mansholt Plan (q.v.) of 1968 was a great step forward in Community thinking on agricultural matters. Became President of the Commission for a period of nine months in 1972 following the unexpected resignation of Franco Malfatti (q.v.), and in this capacity he showed particular concern for public welfare and environmental protection.

Mansholt Plan

A ten year plan for the restructuring of the Community's agriculture. Produced in 1968, it was entitled 'Agriculture 1980,' but is better known as the Mansholt Plan after its originator, Dr Sicco Mansholt (q.v.). The plan proposed a restructuring of agriculture in the E.C. with the aim of improving efficiency and decreasing the high costs of the Common Agricultural Policy (q.v.). The plan proposed greater emphasis on guidance as opposed to guarantee and a halt on price rises for products in structural surplus. Greater agricultural efficiency was to be promoted by increasing the size of holdings, encouraging greater mechanization and taking some 5 million hectares of the poorer land out of cultivation altogether. These measures would all require a considerable decrease in the numbers employed in agriculture and older farmers were to be encouraged, using financial inducements, to leave the land. Parts of the Plan were implemented by a Council decision of 1972, but the problem of high costs and structural surpluses was not fully solved.

Marjolin, Robert

Former member of the Commission. Born Paris 1911 and trained as an economist. Member of de Gaulle's staff during and after the Second World War and in charge of the plan for French economic recovery (Monnet Plan). Became the first Director-General of the Organization for European Economic Cooperation (q.v.). Member and Vice-President of the Commission from 1958 to 1967 with special responsibility for economic and financial affairs. One of the 'Three Wise Men' (q.v.) appointed in 1979 to examine the structure of the Community.

Marshall Plan

Proposal in 1947 by the American Secretary of State, George Marshall, for American financial assistance to put the countries of Europe on their feet economically following the devastation of the Second World War. It was welcomed by the western European countries, but not by the Soviet bloc. In 1948 the Organization for European Economic Cooperation (q.v.) was set up, and between 1948 and 1952 it disbursed some $17000 million in Marshall Aid to 18 European countries. This programme contributed strongly both to the economic recovery of the 1950s and to the will of the European countries to work more closely together.

Mashreq countries

The four Middle Eastern states of Egypt (q.v.), Jordan (q.v.), Lebanon (q.v.) and Syria (q.v.). There are individual cooperation agreements with the E.C. in the fields of trade, economic policy, finance and aid. They are recipients of loans from the European Investment Bank (q.v.) to finance projects in production, infrastructure and training programmes. There is freedom of access for Mashreq exports into the Community, except for those products covered by the Common Agricultural Policy (q.v.) for which there are tariff preferences. A minimum of 'most-favoured-nation' treatment is granted on E.C. exports to the Mashreq countries. A Cooperation Council has been established to oversee the agreements and to promote institutional contacts. The agreements with the Mashreq countries can be seen as part of the Community's overall Mediterranean Policy (q.v.).

Mauritania
West African state signatory of the Yaoundé and Lomé Conventions (q.v.). Former French colony which became independent in 1960.

Mauritius
Small island state in the Indian Ocean signatory of the second Yaoundé Convention (q.v.) and the Lomé Conventions (q.v.). Former British colony which became independent in 1968 and is now a member of the Commonwealth.

Mayer, René
Former President of the High Authority of the European Coal and Steel Community. French political leader who held high office, including that of Prime Minister, in the governments of the French Fourth Republic. An active supporter of moves towards greater European unity, he succeeded Jean Monnet (q.v.) as President of the High Authority in 1955.

Mayne, Dr Richard
Born 1926. Educated at Cambridge University and joined the Staff of the European Coal and Steel Community in 1956 and the European Economic Community in 1958. In 1963 he became Director of Jean Monnet's Action Committee for the United States of Europe and following British membership in 1973 became head of the Community's London Office. In 1979 appointed special adviser to the President of the Commission. Writer and broadcaster on European affairs.

Mediterranean policy
The countries of the Mediterranean basin have always been regarded as being of special importance to the Community and to Western Europe as a whole, for economic, political and strategic reasons. In the early 1960s both Greece and Turkey were given associate status and have since evolved close relations with the Community. Since then an attempt has been made to develop a global policy in relation to the Mediterranean countries. Agreements with similar provisions have been reached with the Maghreb (q.v.) and Mashreq (q.v.) countries and also with Yugoslavia. In general the aim has been to move towards the creation of a free trade area between the E.C. and the non-Community countries of the Mediterranean and to channel Community aid into their economic development.

Mediterranean pollution *see* Barcelona Convention

Mediterranean regions of the Community, development of
In 1978 the Commission published its guidelines for the improvement of agriculture in the Mediterranean regions of the Community. They included irrigation projects, particularly in the Mezzogiorno (q.v.), conversion of vineyards, forestry, improvement of public services and marketing of fruit and vegetables. Arrangements for action based on these guidelines were subsequently adopted by the Council.

Meetings of Foreign Ministers in Political Cooperation
Institution established for the discussion of foreign affairs outside the strict terms of reference of the E.C. Treaties. As a result, common positions have been reached on a variety of international problems and the current president of the Council normally speaks for the Community at international gatherings. *See also* Council of Ministers, Committee of Political Directors.

M.E.P.
Member of the European Parliament. Designation which has become common since the direct elections to the European Parliament in June 1979.

Merger of the Communities
In 1967 the executives of the European Coal and Steel Community, the European Economic Community and the European Atomic Energy Community were replaced by a new 14 member Commission which from then on took charge of the affairs of all three. While the three Communities still exist separately in legal terms, they now operate in almost all respects as a single unit.

Messina Conference
Meeting of the foreign ministers of the six members of European Coal and Steel Community in 1955 in an atmosphere of some gloom following the failure of the European Defence Community (q.v.). The resolution coming from this Conference stated that the time had come to make fresh advances in the building of a united Europe and that this must be achieved first in the economic field.

A committee under the chairmanship of Paul-Henri Spaak (q.v.) was set up to investigate the feasibility of establishing a common market.

Mexico
Signatory of non-preferential agreement with the E.C. for the promotion of economic and commercial cooperation.

Mezzogiorno
The name given to the Italian peninsula south of Rome together with Sicily and Sardina. It covers about two-fifths of the country's area and its population of 19 millions is some 30 per cent of the national total. It is the poorest and least developed part not only of Italy but of the whole Community and from it large numbers of people have migrated to the more prosperous north of the country and to other areas of the Community. The *Cassa per il Mezzogiorno* was set up by the Italian government in 1951 to promote the development of the region and after 1958 it became a major recipient of aid from the E.E.C. funds. These include loans from the European Investment Bank (q.v.), and grants from the European Regional Development Fund (q.v.), and the European Agricultural Guidance and Guarantee Fund (q.v.). The aid has gone into a wide range of industrial and infrastructure projects and into the modernization of agriculture. The result has been a considerable development of industry and the creation of large numbers of new jobs, but the chronic problems of the region are by no means entirely solved.

Migrant workers
There are six million migrant workers in the countries of the Community, but only around a quarter of these come from other E.C. countries themselves. Of these latter the Italians and the Irish are the largest national groups, totalling together well over one million. Those from outside the Community are mainly from the Mediterranean area, in particular Turkey, Portugal, Yugoslavia, Spain and Algeria, and also from the Commonwealth. They have moved from poor countries with high unemployment to find work in the industries of north-west Europe. The country attracting the largest number of migrant workers is the Federal Republic of Germany, followed by France and the United Kingdom. The migrant workers originating in other Community countries now have established economic and social rights. *See also* Freedom of movement of workers.

Milk and milk products
Products regulated under the E.C.'s common organization of the agricultural market. The target price (q.v.) for milk with stipulated fat content is supported by intervention prices. Aids are available for storage of products, for denaturing of surpluses and conversion into animal feedstuffs. There is a levy on imports and export refunds when the world price is below that in the Community. Structural surpluses are lessened through the imposition of a levy on milk sales, suspension of aids to the dairy sector and premiums for the replacement of dairy herds and non-marketing of milk and milk products. *See also* Butter; Cheese.

Monetary and financial policy
The object of this is the coordination of the policies of the member states to the extent needed for the proper economic functioning of the Community. A Committee of Governors of Central Banks has been established to coordinate internal and external monetary policies. The European Monetary Cooperation Fund (q.v.) has the function of raising loans for member states with balance of payments problems. Both Ireland and Italy have received such loans. The European Unit of Account (E.U.A.) — the 'basket of currencies' (q.v.) — has been adopted by the Community's financial institutions for their borrowing and lending operations and is also used in the Community budget. *See also* European Monetary System.

Monetary Compensatory Amounts (M.C.As)
The object of these is to maintain the value of agricultural price guarantees at times of monetary instability and to permit free movement of foodstuffs at fixed prices. M.C.As compensate the difference between market rates of exchange and the representative rates used in price guarantees. They are levied or granted on trade between member states and also on trade with third countries. For countries with revalued currencies they are levied on imports and granted on exports, and for countries with devalued currencies they are levied on exports and

granted on imports. M.C.As became a permanent feature of the Common Agricultural Policy (q.v.) by 1975 with the floating of national currencies and the introduction of the 'green currencies'. It is the policy of the Community to limit the amount spent on the M.C.As and to bring the green currency levels closer to the actual exchange rates.

Monnet, Jean (1888 – 1979) 'The father of Europe'
Born Cognac, France. French civil servant who rose to become the first Deputy Secretary-General of the League of Nations. In this capacity he was active in international economic affairs. In 1940 he proposed Franco-British union and, after the fall of France, became an Anglo-French civil servant in London and Washington. Later he became a member of de Gaulle's government in Algiers, and in 1945 the head of the French Commissariat du Plan in charge of economic strategy for the reconstruction and development of the country. In 1950 he proposed to Robert Schuman (q.v.) the plan for the first of the Communities and this came to fruition in 1952 as the European Coal and Steel Community with Monnet as the first President of its High Authority. He held this position until 1955 and subsequently founded the Action Committee for the United States of Europe. Through this he continued to advocate further integrative measures. He strongly supported the merger of the Communities, enlargement and direct elections to the European Parliament. He was awarded both the Charlemagne (q.v.) and the Schuman Prizes (q.v.) and in 1976 the European Council gave him the title 'Honorary Citizen of Europe' in recognition of his outstanding work towards European unity.

Morocco
North African state signatory of the Maghreb cooperation agreements (q.v.). Specific quotas are laid down for the export to the Community of certain products covered by the Common Agricultural Policy (q.v.).

Mountain and hill farming *see* Hill farming

'Mountains'
The name given to unsold surpluses of foodstuffs bought under the Community's system of intervention buying in order to support price levels. These surpluses have been caused by overproduction arising from the high prices available to farmers for certain products. Dairy produce and beef 'mountains' have appeared at various times and they have been reduced in size by subsidized sales to specific categories of consumers, exports at low prices to third countries and even as animal feedstuffs.

Mugnozza, Carlo Scarascia
Former Vice-President and member of the Commission. Born Rome 1920. Entered politics as a Christian Democrat in 1953 and subsequently held office as Minister of Education and Minister of Justice. Member of the European Parliament from 1962 to 1972. Member of the Commission from 1972 to 1973 in charge of agriculture, and then from 1973 to 1977 as a Vice-President, responsible for a portfolio which included environmental and transport policy, consumer protection and information.

Multifibre Agreements
Bilateral voluntary restraint agreements negotiated between the E.C. and principal exporters of low-cost textiles. These agreements have been made under the all-fibres arrangements of the General Agreement on Tariffs and Trade (q.v.) in order to avoid market disruptions. Under the present arrangement, low-cost imports of particularly sensitive products have been stabilized and there is a limitation on the growth rate for others. The principal exporting countries involved are in South-East Asia and South America.

Mutton and lamb
Products regulated under the Common Agricultural Policy (q.v.). Common organization of the market was established following the 'lamb war' (q.v.) between the United Kingdom and France. Intervention buying takes place at certain times of the year and subsidies are available to finance the difference between the set price and the market price. Guidance premiums are paid under certain conditions to producers of mutton and lamb. The Community market is protected from external competition, principally from New Zealand (q.v.), by limitations on imports into the Community.

N

Narjes, Dr Karl-Heinz

Member of the Commission. Born Soltau 1924 and after war service in the navy educated at the University of Hamburg. Entered the service of the government of the *land* of Bremen and subsequently served in the Federal Ministry of Foreign Affairs. In 1958 was seconded to the European Economic Community and from 1963 to 1968 was *chef de cabinet* to the President of the Commission, and afterwards Director-General of Press and Information. From 1969 to 1973 was Minister for Economics and Business of the *land* of Schleswig-Holstein. Elected to the Bundestag in 1972 and became president of the economic affairs committee. Appointed Commissioner in 1981 with special responsibility for advanced technology.

Natali, Lorenzo

Vice-President of the Commission. Born Florence 1922. Active in the resistance movement during the Second World War and then entered politics as a Christian Democrat. Held office successively as Minister of Finance, the Merchant Navy, Tourism and Entertainment, Public Works and Agriculture. In the latter capacity he was active at Community level in agricultural reform and regional policy. Commissioner since 1977 with special responsibility for enlargement, protection of the environment and nuclear safety, and since 1981 also for relations with the Mediterranean countries.

Netherlands, The

Founder member state of the European Coal and Steel Community, the European Economic Community and the European Atomic Energy Community (q.v.), and member of most other Western organizations. With an area of 41 200 km^2, a population of 13.9 millions and a density of 336 per km^2 – twice the Community average – this is the most densely populated country in the whole of Western Europe. Higher densities still are found in the provinces of North and South Holland, the historic heartland of the country. Here the 'Randstad' conurbation, which includes the major cities of Amsterdam, Rotterdam and the Hague has 40 per cent of the nation's total population. This all reflects the intensity of land-use in this small country having under three per cent of the Community's total area, and such has been the pressure that large areas have been added by reclamation from the sea. The rich agricultural land, and particularly the western polders, has made it one of the most intensively farmed countries in Europe, specializing in the production of vegetables, fruit, flowers and dairy produce. For centuries the Netherlands has also been one of the world's great trading nations and its huge colonial empire in the Dutch East Indies became the independent state of Indonesia in 1949. Rotterdam, together with Europort, is now the largest cargo port in the Community and its vast hinterland stretches down the Rhine to Switzerland. Since the Second World War the country has also industrialized and oil refining, chemicals, petrochemicals, steelmaking and light engineering are of particular importance. The Netherlands has a high level of economic interdependence with its Community partners and they account for over two-thirds of its exports and over a half of its imports. It has usually been one of the greatest supporters of the enlargement of the Community and of all measures leading towards greater European integration. Since 1947 it has been closely associated with Belgium and Luxembourg in the Benelux Union (q.v.).

Neumark Committee
Set up in 1960 under the chairmanship of Fritz Neumark for the purpose of considering the fiscal and financial problems arising out of the common market. Its report advocated a harmonization of Value Added Tax (q.v.) for wholesale only, a separate tax on retail transactions, and the equalization of profits taxes.

New Community Instrument (N.I.C.)
Known more familiarly as the 'Ortoli Facility,' after the Commissioner in charge of economic policy, this is a fund of 1000 million European Units of Account (q.v.) set up by the Community in 1979 for the purpose of providing specific aid to energy and infrastructure projects in the Community. Loans have been allocated for peat-fired power stations in Ireland, a hydroelectric power station in North Wales and the development of geothermal energy in northern Italy. Each project is examined by the Commission which consults with the European Investment Bank (q.v.).

New Zealand
Commonwealth state having close trading relations with the E.C. The Community is New Zealand's largest single market, taking over 30 per cent of the country's exports. Most of this trade is with Britain which has in the past given very favourable treatment to New Zealand exports of butter, cheese and lamb. Following United Kingdom entry into the Community in 1973, the New Zealand economy faced considerable problems, but export quotas of butter and cheese were guaranteed for five years and subsequently the butter quota was extended to 1980.

Next European Torus (N.E.T.)
Projected successor to the Joint European Torus (q.v.).

Niger
West African state signatory of the Yaoundé and Lomé Conventions (q.v.). Former French colony which became fully independent in 1960.

Nigeria
West African state signatory of the Lomé Conventions (q.v.). Former British colony which became independent in 1963 and is now a republic within the Commonwealth.

'Nine, The'
Name given to the nine member countries of the European Communities between the enlargement of 1973 and the accession of Greece in 1981.

Nordic Council
An international grouping consisting of Sweden, Norway, Denmark, Finland and Iceland. It binds these countries together in a framework of cooperation but does not in any way infringe their sovereign rights. Over the years mutually beneficial action has been taken in the administrative, economic and cultural fields. Denmark is the only Nordic Council member which is also a member of the E.C.

Norm price
Price which the producer of tobacco is guaranteed under the Common Agricultural Policy (q.v.). *See also* Target price, Guide price.

North Atlantic Treaty Organization (N.A.T.O.)
A defence alliance of 13 West European states together with the United States and Canada which was established by the Treaty of Washington in 1949. The European countries consist of the members of the Community, except for France and Ireland, together with Norway, Iceland, Portugal and Turkey. France had been a member until 1966 when she withdrew her armed forces from the N.A.T.O. command structure so as to be freer to conduct a more independent foreign policy. She has since continued to maintain contacts with the alliance. The member countries are pledged to provide assistance to any one of their number which is attacked by a third country in Europe, and their armed forces operate in the European theatre under a unified command structure. Each member retains sovereign control over the operation of its own armed forces. While the primary role of the alliance has always been the defence of Western Europe, it has agencies concerned with political, economic and other matters. The headquarters of the

alliance is in Brussels, and the Supreme Headquarters of the N.A.T.O. command (S.H.A.P.E.) is in Mons.

North–South Dialogue
The name given to the Conference on International Economic Cooperation (C.I.E.C.) between 19 developing countries and 17 industrial ones which took place from 1975 to 1977. At this conference the member countries of the E.C. were represented by a single delegation. The purpose of the conference was to consider the establishment of a more equitable organization of international economic relations so as to reduce the imbalances between the developed and the developing countries. Agreements were reached on matters relating to energy and raw materials conservation, and a special action programme was initiated for the purpose of aiding the poorest of the developing countries. It was also agreed that the resources of the International Monetary Fund should be increased and measures taken to encourage greater private investment in the developing countries. A Committee chaired by Willy Brandt (q.v.) was set up to draw up proposals for the reorganization of relations between the developed and the developing world and this reported in 1980. *See also* United Nations Conference on Trade and Development (U.N.C.T.A.D.).

Norway
Scandinavian state signatory of an industrial free trade agreement with the E.C. in 1973 to be implemented over a period of years. Norway had negotiated membership of the Community at the same time as the United Kingdom, Denmark and Ireland, but a popular referendum in 1972 rejected this and the country remained outside.It is a member of both the Nordic Council (q.v.) and the European Free Trade Association (q.v.), and it was as a member of the latter that the trade agreement with the Community was negotiated. About a half of the country's total external trade is now conducted with the Community, her principal exports being primary products such as oil, wood and fish.

Nuclear policy *see* European Atomic Energy Community

O

Oils and oil seeds *see* Vegetable oils and fats

O'Kennedy, Michael
Member of the Commission. Born 1936 in County Tipperary and educated at the National University of Ireland. Called to the Bar in 1957. Elected Fianna Fáil member of the Seanad in 1965 and the Dáil Eireann in 1969. Held the offices of Minister of Transport, Finance and Foreign Affairs. Appointed Commissioner in 1981 with special responsibility for personnel, consumer affairs, environment and as a delegate of the President.

Organization for Economic Cooperation and Development (O.E.C.D.)
Intergovernmental organization which in 1961 replaced the Organization for European Economic Cooperation (q.v.). Unlike its predecessor it is not confined to Europe, and in addition to the former O.E.E.C. members and Finland, the United States, Canada, Japan, Australia and New Zealand have joined. Yugoslavia has associate status. The aims of the organization, like those of its predecessor, are the liberalization of trade, the encouragement of economic growth and consultation on monetary and fiscal policies. Aid is also available for member countries experiencing economic difficulties. The Community works closely with O.E.C.D. and participates, on a non-voting basis, in its specialist committees.

Organization for European Economic Cooperation (O.E.E.C.)
Intergovernmental organization established in 1948 for the purpose of channelling American 'Marshall Aid' to the countries of Western Europe (see Marshall Plan). Originally there were 16 member countries, but this eventually grew to 18. They included all the present members of the Community together with Norway, Sweden, Iceland, Spain, Portugal, Switzerland, Austria and Turkey. After the end of the American aid programme in 1953 the O.E.E.C. continued as an organization concerned with the liberalization of trade, the encouragement of economic growth and consultation on monetary and fiscal policies. In 1961 it was replaced by the Organization for Economic Cooperation and Development (q.v.).

Ortoli, François-Xavier
Member and former President of the Commission. Born 1925 in Ajaccio, Corsica and educated in French Indo-China and at the Ecole Nationale d'Administration. Civil servant in the Ministry of Finance and Economic Development and in 1958 became Director-General for the Internal Market and the Harmonization of Laws in the E.C. Returned to French government service, became head of the National Planning Commission and in 1968 was elected to the National Assembly. Held office successively as Minister of Public Works, Education, Economic Affairs and Finance, and Industrial and Scientific Development. President of the Commission from 1973 to 1977 during

which time the Community had to cope with enlargement and mounting economic crisis. Subsequently Vice-President of the Commission since 1977 in charge of economic affairs, finance, credits and investments.

Ortoli Facility *see* New Community Instrument

Overseas Countries and Territories (O.C.T.)
When the Treaty of Rome (q.v.) was signed in 1957, members of the E.C. (6) had large overseas possessions and special economic arrangements were made for them. They were given privileged access to the Community market and received financial assistance. Within a few years many of them had become independent states and the Yaoundé Convention (q.v.) was negotiated with these. Separate arrangements were made for the remainder of the overseas possessions, and following enlargement in 1973 this was also applied to those of the United Kingdom. Under agreed arrangements freedom of access is guaranteed for O.C.T. exports into the Community market except for those products covered by the Common Agricultural Policy (q.v.) for which there are special provisions. Quotas have also been agreed for O.C.T. exports of cane sugar. In return a minimum of 'most-favoured-nation' treatment is granted on E.C. exports, there being no discrimination among Community countries. The STABEX price guarantee system (q.v.) negotiated under the Lomé Conventions (q.v.), is also applied. Loans are provided by the European Investment Bank (q.v.) and aid by the European Development Fund (q.v.), the former in equal parts to the British, Dutch and French territories. Over 20 territories now have O.C.T. status, among the most important being French Somaliland, Belize, Brunei and the Associated States in the Caribbean. When O.C.T. members become fully independent, they may apply for accession to the Lomé Convention.

P

Pakistan
Commonwealth state in the Indian subcontinent. Signatory with the E.C. of a bilateral voluntary restraint agreement on the export of textile products under the Multifibre Agreements (q.v.). A non-preferential commercial cooperation agreement is also in force.

Papua New Guinea
Western Pacific state signatory to the Lomé Conventions (q.v.). Former Australian mandated territory which became independent in 1975 and is now a member of the Commonwealth.

Paris
Capital city of France and major international centre. With a population of 10 millions, Greater Paris is one of the largest cities in the whole of the Community and is the centre of France's political, economic and cultural life. It is the headquarters of a number of international bodies including the Organization for European Cooperation and Development (q.v.) and the United Nations Educational, Social and Cultural Organization (UNESCO).

Paris Convention
International Convention for the prevention of marine pollution from land-based sources. Signed by the E.C. in 1975.

Paris, Treaty of
Signed in 1951 by France, the Federal Republic of Germany, Italy, Belgium, the Netherlands and Luxembourg, this treaty set up the European Coal and Steel Community. It had a term of 50 years and was open to any other European country. The signature of this treaty was a great step forward in the reconciliation of the countries of western Europe after the Second World War, and the preamble states that the contracting parties were 'resolved to substitute for historic rivalries a fusion of their essential interests, to establish, by creating an economic community, the foundations of a broader and deeper community among peoples long divided by bloody conflicts.' Following the signature of the treaty, the 'Six' went on to explore other avenues of international cooperation and six years later they were to sign the Treaty of Rome (q.v.).

Parliament *see* European Parliament

Patents *see* European Patent Convention

Paul Finet Foundation
Established in 1965 by the High Authority of the European Coal and Steel Community in honour of one of its former presidents. It provides educational grants for orphans of workers in the coal, iron and steel industries who died as a direct consequence of their occupation. Priority goes to those orphans suffering real financial hardships and renewal is conditional upon good academic performance.

Permanent Representatives *see* Committee of Permanent Representatives

Petten
Town in the Netherlands which is the location of one of the four nuclear research establishments set up by the European Atomic Energy Community. It is now part of the Joint Research Centre (q.v.).

Pflimlin, Pierre
French political leader and Mayor of Strasbourg. Born 1907 in Roubaix. President of the Mouvement Républicain Populaire from 1956 to 1959. Prime Minister immediately prior to the assumption of power by de Gaulle (q.v.) in 1958. President of the Consultative Assembly of the Council of Europe (q.v.) from 1963 to 1965 and European People's Party member of the European Parliament since 1979.

Philippines
State in the Western Pacific signatory of bilateral voluntary restraint agreements on the export of textile products to the E.C. under the Multifibre Agreements (q.v.).

Pigmeat
Includes pork, bacon and other pigmeat products and all are subject to price determination under the Common Agricultural Policy (q.v.). Levies are imposed on imports if necessary and there is buying by intervention agencies when the price falls below the agreed level. Aid is provided for private storage of unsold stocks, and export refunds are made to enable producers to export when world prices are below the E.C. target price.

Pisani, Edgard
Member of the Commission. Born Tunis 1918 and educated at Tunis and Paris. As a civil servant he rose to become a sub-prefect, prefect and *chef de cabinet* in a number of ministries during the Fourth Republic. Entered politics in 1954 as Senator for Haute-Marne and later became Deputy for Maine-et-Loire. Held office from 1962 to 1967 successively as Minister of Agriculture, Equipment and Housing. Appointed Commissioner in 1981 to replace Claude Cheysson (q.v.) with special responsibility for aid and development.

Pleven Plan *see* European Defence Community

Political Groups in the European Parliament
A group consists of a body of Members of the European Parliament (q.v.) having the same or similar political ideas who consequently agree to constitute a party at European level. The minimum strength for an official group is 14, or 10 from at least three different member states. They may be relatively loose alliances compared to national parties, but groups have financial and other benefits which are not available to non-attached members. During plenary sessions of the European Parliament the members sit according to political group rather than nationality. The seven political groups in the European Parliament elected in 1979 are, in order of size, the Socialists (q.v.), European People's Party (q.v.), European Democrats (q.v.), Communists (q.v.), Liberals (q.v.), European Progressive Democrats (q.v.) and the Group for the Technical Coordination and Defence of Independent Groups and Members. There are only nine non-attached members.

Pollution
Mediterranean *see* Barcelona Convention, Rhine *see* Rhine.

Portugal
European state which signed a preferential trade agreement with the E.C. in 1973. This followed the entry into the Community of Britain, Denmark and Ireland and the subsequent negotiation of trade agreements with the remaining members of the European Free Trade Association (q.v.) which included Portugal. There is also an agreement giving Portuguese workers in the Community social security and medical benefits. An industrial and technical cooperation agreement is in force and financial aid is provided in the form of loans from the European Investment Bank (q.v.). Portugal is an applicant for full membership of the Community, and negotiations to this end have been taking place since 1978.

Poultrymeat
There is no fixed price system in this commodity but measures are in force to improve

production and marketing and to monitor price trends. There is protection of the industry by variable levies and export refunds on exports if world prices are lower than the E.C. price.

Prag, Derek
Born 1923 and educated Cambridge University. European civil servant and former Head of the London Office of the European Communities. Since 1979 European Member of Parliament for Hertfordshire. Economic journalist and industrial consultant on European affairs.

Preferences *see* Generalized System of Preferences

Progressive Democrats *see* European Progressive Democrats

R

Reference price

The minimum price at which an agricultural product may be imported from a non-member country. Similar to the sluice-gate price (q.v.) but applying to fruit and vegetables, wines and certain fish products. *See also* Common Agricultural Policy.

Referendums on membership of the European Communities

These were held in Denmark, Ireland, Norway and the United Kingdom following the signature of the Treaty of Accession (*see* Accession, Treaties of) by these four countries in 1972. In the first three of these it was decided that the final decision on membership must be made by popular vote. In the referendums subsequently held there was a 'Yes' vote in Ireland of 83 per cent and in Denmark 63 per cent. In Norway, however, there was a 53 per cent vote against, and as a consequence the country did not become a member. The referendum in the United Kingdom was not held until 1975, following a change of government, the new Labour administration having pledged itself to seek popular approval for membership. The government advised continued membership and 67 per cent of the electorate voted in favour of this. In France also there was referendum to approve enlargement and a majority voted in favour of this.

Regional development policy

Concern for balanced regional development has from the outset been an important part of Community thinking, and in the Treaty of Rome (q.v.) there is specific reference to the need for this. The aim was seen as being to ensure that all parts of the Community had a share in the prosperity which it helped to create and to give special assistance to the poorest regions. Subsequently many of the policies pursued by the Community had important regional aspects, and the activities of the European Investment Bank (q.v.) were particularly directed towards the less favoured regions. In 1973 the Report on Regional Problems in the Enlarged Community (Thomson Report) (q.v.) outlined the task as being principally to support backward regions, reduce the hold of the great centrally located conurbations, coordinate existing Community policies and help the regional activities of the more hard-pressed national governments. The most concrete result of this was the establishment of the European Regional Development Fund (q.v.) in 1975.

Regional Fund *see* European Regional Development Fund

Regulation

A decision taken by Council as the legislative body of the European Communities. This then has the force of law throughout the E.C. It has general application and confers obligations and entitlements directly on the member states and on their citizens. *See also* Directive.

Relance
Name given to the 'relaunching' of the ideal of European unity after a period of setbacks and stagnation. Such regaining of the initiative is associated with the period following the Messina Conference (q.v.) in 1955 and again after the Hague Summit (q.v.) in 1969.

Republic of Ireland *see* Ireland, Republic of

Rey, Jean
Former member and president of the Commission. Born Liège, Belgium in 1902 and educated at the University of Liège. Entered politics as a Liberal in 1939 and, after imprisonment during the Second World War, served as Minister of Reconstruction and of Economic Affairs in post-war Belgian governments. With the establishment of the European Economic Community in 1958 he was appointed Commissioner with special responsibility for external relations and was leader of the Community delegation in the Kennedy Round (q.v.) negotiations. With the merger of the Communities in 1967, he became President of the new Commission, a post which he retained until 1970. He subsequently served as a member of the European Parliament and after direct elections in 1979 became a member of the Liberal Group in the European Parliament. He chaired the committee which in 1980 produced the Rey Report (q.v.) on Community institutions.

Rey Report
A report which appeared in 1980 of a committee set up by the European Parliament and chaired by Jean Rey (q.v.). The object was to review the workings of the Community institutions and to consider ways in which these could be improved. The main recommendations in the Report were that the Commission should play a more political role, that Parliament should have a say in the appointment of the President of the Commission, that the Commission should submit its proposed policies annually to a Parliamentary vote and that it should liaise with Parliament before its proposals are submitted to Council. Advisory bodies should remain advisory and not attempt to usurp the Commission's role and women should be 'adequately represented' on the Commission.

Rhine, pollution problems
For an international river running through five countries there are special problems in controlling pollution. The Commission participates as an observer in the International Commission for the Protection of the Rhine against Pollution (I.C.P.R.) and is a signatory of the Berne Convention for the protection of the Rhine against chemical pollution.

Rice
Product subject to price determination under the Common Agricultural Policy (q.v.). Target and intervention prices and special intervention measures are used as necessary. Export refunds are made to enable producers to export when world prices are below the Community target price, and this may be replaced by a levy in case of shortage within the Community.

Richard, Ivor
Member of the Commission. Born Cardiff in 1932 and educated Oxford University. Called to the Bar in 1955 and entered politics in 1964 as Labour M.P. for Baron's Court. Held minor office in the Labour government of 1964–1970. Permanent British representative to the United Nations from 1974 to 1979, during which time he chaired the 1976 Rhodesia Conference. Became a Commissioner in 1981 with special responsibility for social affairs.

Rights of establishment and freedom to provide services
These rights are provided for under the Treaty of Rome (q.v.). The right of establishment anywhere within the Community by Community nationals and Community firms has been implemented. For this purpose restrictions have been abolished on residence in other member states and on the transfer of funds for the purpose of establishment. Provision of services by Community nationals in other member states is subject to agreement on the mutual acceptance of professional and other qualifications. Acceptance has been agreed upon in the wholesale and retail trades, insurance, real estate, films, banking, law, the medical profession, dentistry, veterinary surgery, nursing and road haulage. Work is progressing in other areas with the aim of eventually liberalising all services by Community nationals taking place within the Community.

Rippon, Geoffrey

British Conservative politician born 1924. Minister in charge of the negotiations for British entry into the European Community in 1970–1971. Member of the European Parliament from 1973 to 1979 and, following the death of Sir Peter Kirk (q.v.), leader of the British Conservatives in the European Parliament from 1977 on.

Rome, Treaties of

The two treaties signed in Rome in March 1957 by Belgium, the Federal Republic of Germany, France, Italy, Luxembourg and the Netherlands. These provided for the establishment of the European Economic Community (E.E.C.) and the European Atomic Energy Community (E.A.E.C. or Euratom). They were the result of discussions to find ways of pursuing the unifying processes which had been so successfully begun with the European Coal and Steel Community six years earlier. The Rome conference which commenced in January 1957 produced the agreed framework within which the new organizations were to operate. The Treaty establishing the E.E.C. has 248 articles and is for the most part a wide-ranging scheme for the integration of the economies of the six signatories over an agreed period of time. It provides for the creation of a customs union in successive stages together with a common external tariff (Articles 9 to 30). This was to apply to all goods in intra-Community trade with the exception of agricultural produce for which there was to be special provision (Articles 38 to 47). There was to be progressive freeing of the movement of persons, services and capital (Articles 48 to 73) and common rules were laid down for financial and commercial conduct. Provision was also made for the development of policies in the transport, social and general economic fields. Since a number of the signatories were still colonial powers, special economic arrangements were made for the Overseas Countries and Territories (q.v.). Institutions were established to run and control the Community and the executive body, the Commission, was provisionally located in Brussels. While the Treaty deals almost entirely with economic matters, the underlying aims were wider and the preamble states that the contracting parties were 'determined to establish the foundations of an ever closer union among the European peoples.' A great deal of what was agreed to in the Treaty has now been implemented in one way or another and an advanced level of economic integration has been reached. Although in many ways now outdated and supplemented by new policies and methods of cooperation, the Treaty of Rome still constitutes the legal basis for the activities of the E.E.C.

The Euratom Treaty signed at the same time established the Atomic Energy Community along similar lines. It provided for the control of nuclear power and research by an international body above the member states. Its success has been limited by the fact that the signatories were not prepared for the total internationalization of something of such potential political and economic significance. Following ratification by the six national parliaments, the Treaties of Rome came into operation in January 1958. In 1972 Denmark, Ireland and the United Kingdom signed and subsequently ratified a Treaty of Accession (*see* Accession, Treaties of), and in 1979 Greece did the same thing. This bound the new members to accept and abide by the provisions of the Treaties of Rome.

Ruhr, The

Large West German coalfield on which the country's most important heavy industrial region is situated. This region was central to the economic strength of Germany during the first half of the twentieth century and as such became an object of fear to neighbouring countries. This was particularly so in the case of France which increasingly saw it as the heart of the Geman power which threatened her. After both World Wars attempts were made to bring it under some form of international control, but these proved impractical and the problem was finally solved by the establishment of the European Coal and Steel Community. This brought the heavy industries of the Federal Republic of Germany into a supranational framework together with those of France and neighbouring countries.

Rwanda

Central African state signatory of the Yaoundé and Lomé Conventions (q.v.). Formerly part of the Belgian trusteeship territories of Ruanda-Urundi which became independent in 1962.

S

Saarland

Small West German *land* adjacent to the frontiers with France and Luxembourg. It possesses an important coalfield, and it was largely to secure this resource that it was partially integrated economically with France after the First World War. It was fully returned to Germany following the referendum of 1935. After the Second World War it was once more occupied by France, but in 1957 was finally returned to the Federal Republic as part of a general agreement which included the canalization of the Moselle river. The political side of the problems associated with the Saarland was largely solved with the establishment of the European Coal and Steel Community.

Saar-Lor-Lux

The 'three state triangle' of Saarland, Lorraine and Luxembourg. Centered on the Moselle river and its tributaries this is a natural geographical unit whose unity, according to Robert Schuman (q.v.), has always been prevented by its history. Now an attempt is being made to break down the divisions created by national frontiers and this is proving possible in the modern climate of cooperation. A development plan has been produced with E.C. funds and there is close cooperation in transport planning and in industrial and agricultural development.

St. Vincent and the Grenadines

Caribbean state signatory of the Lomé Conventions (q.v.). British colony which became independent in 1979 and is now a member of the Commonwealth.

Saint-Geours Report

Report which appeared in 1979 by a group of independent experts from E.C. countries entitled 'Energy-efficient growth.' It stressed the need to dissociate economic growth from energy consumption and to this end proposed the harmonization of energy policies. Specific proposals were the making of energy costs more transparent, research on energy conservation technology and the introduction of common standards of technical performance.

São Thomé and Principe

Small island state off the west coast of Africa signatory of the Lomé Conventions (q.v.). Former Portuguese colony which became independent in 1975.

Schaus Memorandum

Produced by the Commission in 1961 and named after Lambert Schaus, the Commissioner at the time responsible for transport. It laid down the general principles for the development of a common E.C. policy on transport.

Schuman, Robert (1886 – 1963)

French statesman and a founder of the European Community. Born into an Alsatian family living in Luxembourg, Schuman entered politics in 1919 as a moderate conservative in the French Chamber of Deputies. After the liberation in 1944 he joined the liberal Catholic party, the Mouvement Républicain Populaire (M.R.P.) and subsequently served as Foreign Minister and

Prime Minister in post-war French governments. It was as Foreign Minister from 1948 to 1953 that he proved to be a passionate advocate of European integration, and in 1950, in cooperation with Jean Monnet (q.v.), was the author of the Schuman Plan (q.v.). This was to lead to the establishment of the European Coal and Steel Community in the following year. He then went on to promote the idea of the European Defence Community (q.v.) but this radical project was eventually defeated in the Chamber of Deputies. Schuman was a member of the European Parliament and remained so until shortly before his death.

Schuman Declaration *see* Schuman Plan

Schuman Plan
Initiative by the French Foreign Minister in 1950 which was to lead to the resolution of the Franco-German conflict which had bedevilled the international situation in Europe for so long. The French fear was of a revived and possibly rearmed Germany and the growing strength of the new Federal Republic of Germany (q.v.) meant that time was running out for the introduction of effective measures of restraint. The plan itself was drawn up by Jean Monnet (q.v.) and submitted to Schuman who was enthusiastic about it. It was unveiled to the world in the 'Schuman Declaration' of May 9th, 1950 and its novel approach and stirring language quickly caught the imagination. 'Europe will not be built all at once,' it said, 'nor through a single comprehensive plan. It will be built through concrete achievements, which will first create a 'de facto' solidarity. The comity of European nations requires that the rivalry between France and Germany should be eliminated. Action should therefore first be concentrated on France and Germany.' The main proposal was to put the French and German iron and steel industries under a single 'High Authority' and this was to be a common basis for development. 'The solidarity between the two countries established by joint production will show that a war between France and Germany becomes not only unthinkable but materially impossible.' The arrangement was to be open to all other European countries who wished to join it. The concept was a functionalist one and so appealed to many for whom the more grandiose federalist solution was unacceptable. Germany immediately accepted the idea, as did Italy and the Benelux countries. The British were not prepared to come in, and the following year the 'Six' went ahead and signed the Treaty of Paris (q.v.) establishing the European Coal and Steel Community.

Schuman Prizes
Two separate prizes awarded annually by the University of Bonn and the Association of the Friends of Robert Schuman to honour those who have made a special contribution to the cause of European unity. Past recipients include such eminent names as Jean Monnet (q.v.), Sicco Mansholt (q.v.), Walter Hallstein (q.v.), Paul-Henri Spaak (q.v.) and Denis de Rougement (q.v.).

Scott, George
Head of the London Office of the European Communities. Born 1926 and educated at the University of Oxford. A former journalist and B.B.C. Television presenter, he was appointed to the London Office in 1979. Writer on historical and international subjects.

Scott-Hopkins, Sir James
Leader of the European Democratic Group (q.v.) in the European Parliament. Born Oxfordshire 1921 and educated Oxford and Cambridge Universities. Entered politics in 1967 as Conservative M.P. for West Derbyshire and in 1973 became one of the British Conservatives in the European Parliament. Elected Conservative member of the European Parliament for Hereford and Worcester in the direct elections of 1979 and became leader of the European Democrats.

Segré Report
Report produced for the Commission in 1966 on the development of the European capital market. It analysed the causes of current weaknesses and favoured fixed rates of exchange in order to help correct these.

Senegal
West African state signatory of the Yaoundé and Lomé Conventions (q.v.). Former French colony which became independent in 1958.

'Seven, The' *see* European Free Trade Association

Seychelles
Island state in the Indian Ocean signatory of the Lomé Conventions (q.v.). Former British colony which became a republic within the Commonwealth in 1976.

Sheep meat *see* Mutton and lamb

Shonfield, Sir Andrew (1917 – 1981)
British writer and academic. Born Surrey and educated Oxford University. Journalist specializing in financial and economic affairs. Member of the committee which produced the Vedel Report (q.v.) from 1971 to 1972, and Director of the Royal Institute of International Affairs from 1972 to 1977. Professor of Economics at the European University Institute (q.v.) from 1978 to 1981. Author of a number of works on European, economic and international affairs.

Sierra Leone
West African state signatory of the Lomé Conventions (q.v.). Former British colony which became independent in 1961 and is now a republic within the Commonwealth.

Simonet, Henri
Former member and Vice-President of the Commission. Born Brussels 1931 and educated at the Free University of Brussels where he subsequently taught. Between 1961 and 1965 was *chef de cabinet* to a number of Belgian government ministers. Entered politics in 1966 as a Socialist and in 1972 was appointed Minister of Economic Affairs. Member of the Commission from 1973 to 1977 with special responsibility for financial matters, energy policy and Euratom.

'Six, The'
Name given to the original six countries which signed the Treaty of Paris in 1951 establishing the European Coal and Steel Community. They were France, the Federal Republic of Germany, Italy, Belgium, the Netherlands and Luxembourg, and six years later these same countries signed the Treaties of Rome establishing the European Economic Community and the European Atomic Energy Community.

Sluice-gate price
Cost price of pigmeat, eggs and poultrymeat produced in those non-member countries with the highest levels of efficiency. An additional amount is added to the levies on products imported into the Community at below this price so as to prevent import of products at below the sum of the sluice-gate price and the protective levy. *See also* Common Agricultural Policy.

'Snake, The'
Agreement by the member states of the E.C. to limit fluctuations in their exchange rates to a narrow band of 2.25 per cent from their central rates. Central banks were to intervene as necessary to keep currencies within the agreed band. The agreement came into force in 1972 and was joined by Norway and Sweden as 'associates.' The only Community country not to join was Italy, but after enlargement in 1973 the United Kingdom and the Irish Republic also opted against membership. Following the withdrawal of France in 1976, it ceased to be in any sense a Community agreement and by 1978 the 'Snake' members numbered only the Federal Republic of Germany, Denmark, Norway and Benelux. It was superseded in 1979 by the European Monetary System (q.v.). During the period of its operation the Snake did limit intra-Community fluctuations and the currencies of member countries floated up and down together against the dollar within an agreed 'Tunnel.'

Soames, Lord (Formerly Sir Christopher Soames)
Former member and Vice-President of the Commission. Born 1920 at Penn, Buckinghamshire and educated Sandhurst. Commissioned into the Coldstream Guards and served during the Second World War in North Africa and Italy. Entered politics in 1950 as Conservative M.P. for Bedford and in 1960 became Minister of Agriculture, Fisheries and Food in which capacity he was actively involved in the negotiations for Britain's entry into the E.C. In 1968 he became ambassador to France at a particularly sensitive period in Anglo-French relations and paved the way for British membership of the Community. He was Commissioner from 1973 to 1977 with special responsibility for external relations. In 1980 he was the last British governor of Rhodesia before it became the independent state of Zimbabwe (q.v.).

Socialist Group
One of the seven party groups in the European Parliament. In the direct elections of 1979 it won 113 seats, making it the largest of all the groups. Its members are drawn from every country in the Community, the largest numbers coming from Federal Republic of Germany (35), France (22), and the United Kingdom (18).

Somalia
East African state signatory of the Yaoundé and Lomé Conventions (q.v.). Union of the former British Somaliland protectorate and the Italian trust territory of Somalia, it became independent in 1960.

Spaak, Paul-Henri (1899 – 1972)
Belgian statesman and active protagonist of European unity. Born Schaerbeek, Belgium and entered politics as a Socialist member of the Belgian parliament in 1932. In 1938 became Belgium's first socialist Prime Minister and during the Second World War was Foreign Minister in the Belgian government-in-exile in London. After the war he presided over the General Assembly of the United Nations, and once more became Belgian Prime Minister and Foreign Minister. From 1949 to 1951 he was President of the Consultative Assembly of the Council of Europe (q.v.) and from 1957 to 1961 was Secretary-General of the North Atlantic Treaty Organization (q.v.). He was appointed by the Messina Conference (q.v.) to chair a committee set up to investigate new ways of moving forward to European unity and the resulting Spaak Report (q.v.) was the basis for the Treaties of Rome (q.v.).

Spaak Report
Report of an intergovernmental committee of the 'Six' (q.v.) set up in 1955 by the Messina Conference (q.v.) under the chairmanship of Paul-Henri Spaak (q.v.). Its remit was to consider 'a fresh advance towards the building of Europe.' The committee's Report stated that this should be in the economic field and that it should take the form of a full customs union rather than a free trade area. It also proposed that development of nuclear energy should be integrated under international control. The report was accepted by the Council in 1956 and was the basis for the Treaties of Rome in the following year.

Spierenburg Report
Report in 1980 of an independent body appointed by the Commission under the chairmanship of Dirk Spierenburg, formerly Vice-President of the High Authority of the European Coal and Steel Community, to examine the Commission's organization and structure. It recommended that in future there should be one Commissioner for each member country, that the number of portfolios should be reduced and that the powers of each Commissioner's 'cabinet' should be restricted. It also suggested improvements in staff deployment, the merging of Directorates-General and greater powers for the Directors-General themselves.

Spinelli, Altiero
Former member of the Commission. Born Rome 1907 and educated at Rome University. A Communist, he took part in the resistance during the Fascist period and was imprisoned. In 1943 founded the European Federalist Movement (q.v.) and later became its Italian Secretary-General. Subsequently Director of the Institute of International Affairs in Rome. Commissioner from 1970 to 1977 in charge of industrial and technological policy and since then has been a member of the European Parliament. Deeply committed to the ideal of European unity and author of a number of books on the subject.

STABEX (Stabilisation of export earnings)
Method by which the E.C. compensates the signatory states of the Lomé Convention (q.v.) for any shortfall in their income from exports of primary products to the Community. In order to qualify for reimbursement the product must have represented at least 7.5 per cent of total exports in the previous year and have fallen by at least 7.5 per cent from the previous four year export average. These requirements are reduced to 2.25 per cent for the poorest states. The appropriation for this purpose is part of the aid allocated to the signatories and takes the form of interest-free loans. In the case of the poorest states it takes the form of outright grants.

Steel policy
Steel was one of the first products to come in for international regulation through the European Coal and Steel Community. It has

long been central to the economies of the majority of Community members and output increased rapidly from the 1950s on as a result of demand created by the buoyant industrial growth. Between 1962 and 1973 production rose from 93 to 150 million tonnes, but in 1974, as a result of the economic crisis, there was a slump and by 1977 production was down to 126 million tonnes. This situation had repercussions throughout the Community and the Commission introduced anti-crisis measures including trade surveillance, anti-dumping rules, fixed reference prices and monitoring of agreements with third countries. Finance has also been provided for retraining schemes, relocation costs and income supplements. The steel crisis is now seen as a chronic one stemming from both recession at home and from cheap steel on the world markets and it requires a long-term approach to its solution. The Commission's thinking on this is contained in the Davignon Plan (q.v.) which envisages dealing with the situation using both commercial and industrial means.

Stella programme
Research involving the European Space Agency in Paris, the European Organization for Nuclear Research in Geneva and the European Commission in Brussels for the purpose of developing high speed data transmission systems. Electronic data is sent from C.E.R.N. (European Centre for Nuclear Research (q.v.)) to a number of European research laboratries via the European Space Agency's orbital test satellite.

Stockholm Convention
Convention signed in 1959 by Austria, Denmark, Norway, Portugal, Sweden, Switzerland and the United Kingdom establishing the European Free Trade Association (q.v.). The signatories agreed to the establishment of an industrial free trade area among them over a ten year period. There was to be no common external tariff and arrangements for agricultural products were to be subject to bilateral negotiation. The signatories also agreed to ensure that free trade was not distorted by subsidies, discrimination against their nationals or restrictive business practices. The free trade area came into force in 1966, four years ahead of schedule.

'Stopping the clock'
Procedure adopted on occasion by the Council under which a specific time is agreed upon for reaching certain policy decisions. If there is no agreement by the specified time then the meeting remains in session for as long as is necessary to reach one. As a result of the use of this tactic, Council had a number of marathon sessions on agricultural questions during the 1960s.

Strasbourg
French city now one of the meeting places of the European Parliament. Located near the Rhine in Alsace it is on the border between France and Germany and has a population of 250000. It has been at the centre of the territorial dispute between the two countries, and from 1871 to 1945 changed hands six times. In 1949 it was chosen to be the meeting place of the new Council of Europe (q.v.) and subsequently was also used by the European Parliament. Since 1979 the directly elected Parliament has sat in the Council of Europe's new building. Strasbourg has now become one of the symbols of European unity and in particular of the reconciliation between France and Federal Republic of Germany.

Stresa Conference
Conference of E.E.C. ministers and representatives from the farming industry in the 'Six' (q.v.) which met in 1958 to consider the special problems of agriculture in the context of the Community's activities. General principles were agreed upon for the setting up of a Common Agricultural Policy (q.v.).

Stresemann, Gustav (1878 – 1929)
German Chancellor and Foreign Minister from 1923 to 1929. Worked for an improvement in the international situation in Europe, and in particular for collaboration between Germany and France. Actively supported the scheme of Aristide Briand (q.v.) for a united states of Europe. Awarded the Nobel Peace Prize jointly with Briand in 1926.

Sudan
East African state signatory of the Lomé Conventions (q.v.). Formerly the condominium of Anglo-Egyptian Sudan, it became an independent state in 1956.

Sugar
International trade in sugar is governed by the International Sugar Agreements. The Community is both an importer and an exporter of sugar and is concerned to secure the markets of the traditional exporting countries of the world. The Commission has acted for the Community as a whole in all negotiations and has acceded to the Agreements subject to negotiations of 'special conditions'. *See also* Sugar Protocol.

Sugar Protocol
The Sugar Protocol to the Lomé Conventions (q.v.) gives the producer states access to the markets of the Community on a quota basis.

Super Sara project *see* Joint Research Centre

Surinam
South American state signatory of the Lomé Conventions (q.v.). Formerly Dutch Guiana, it became independent in 1975.

Swaziland
State in southern Africa signatory of the Lomé Conventions (q.v.). Former British High Commission Territory which became independent in 1968 and is now a member of the Commonwealth.

Sweden
Scandinavian state signatory of industrial free trade agreement with the E.C. in 1973 and implemented over a period of years. Sweden is a member of both the Nordic Council (q.v.) and the European Free Trade Association (q.v.) and it was as a member of the latter that her trade agreement was negotiated following the enlargement of the Community to include two E.F.T.A. members. A half of the country's total external trade is now conducted with the Community, her principal exports being transport equipment, metallurgical goods and primary materials, in particular wood and iron ore.

Switzerland
Neutral European state signatory of an industrial free trade agreement with the E.C. in 1973 and implemented over a period of years. Switzerland is a member of the European Free Trade Association (q.v.) and it was as such that the industrial free trade agreement was negotiated following the enlargement of the Community to include two former E.F.T.A. members. Over a half of the country's total external trade is with the Community, her principal exports being watches, precision equipment and food products. There is a transit agreement for Community goods crossing Swiss territory.

Syria
Middle Eastern state having cooperation agreements with the E.C. as part of the general agreement with the Mashreq (q.v.) countries. Recipient of loans from the European Investment Bank (q.v.).

T

Tachograph
Mechanical equipment which in accordance with Community regulation must be carried in road transport vehicles for recording distance travelled, vehicle speed, driving time, breaks from work and daily rest periods. *See also* Transport Policy.

Tanzania
East African state signatory of the Arusha and Lomé Conventions (q.v.). Consists of the former British protectorates of Tanganyika and Zanzibar which were united in 1964, and is now a republic within the Commonwealth.

Target price
Price which the producer of certain agricultural products is guaranteed under the Common Agricultural Policy (q.v.). The products covered are cereals, sugar, milk, olive oil, and colza and sunflower seeds. *See also* Guide price.

Tariffs *see* General Agreement on Tariffs and Trade

Taxation, harmonization of
Under the Community treaties, an important object is the harmonization of all tax laws in the member states. This is basically to prevent distortion of competition and restriction of the free movement of goods, services and capital. The Community has already moved some way in this direction. In indirect taxation, Value Added Tax (q.v.) has been introduced throughout the Community. The requirement is in force that taxes on goods from other member states are not to exceed those on similar domestic products and that repayments of internal taxation on exported goods are not to exceed direct or indirect internal taxation in the importing country. Special exemptions from V.A.T. and excise duties are in operation for those travelling within the Community. Work is now in progress on the direct taxation of companies operating in more than one Community country and on the avoidance of double tax by Community companies involved in mergers. This is all related to the European Company Law (q.v.). It is aimed to bring about the harmonization of Value Added Tax and Excise duties levied in the different member states. *See also* Excise duty.

Ten, The
Collective name given to the member states of the Community following Greek accession in 1981. It was temporarily used after the signing of the Treaties of Accession (q.v.) in 1972 by the United Kingdom, Denmark, Ireland and Norway, but had to be dropped when Norway rejected membership after a referendum.

Textile industry policy
In recent years the textile industries of the Community countries have faced many problems caused both by structural difficulties and by competition from third countries. In 1971 the Community produced its guidelines for the reorganization of the industry. Action

was planned at Community level on restructuring, financing and the use of the European Social Fund (q.v.) for conversion and retraining schemes. Action to aid the industry is also seen as part of the Community's wider regional plolicy. There are market restrictions and agreements have been reached on the control of the international textile trade. Bilateral agreements have been made limiting the imports of textile products from certain developing countries. (*see* Multifibre Agreements).

Thailand
Far Eastern state signatory of agreements with the E.C. on trade in certain textile products. There is a bilateral voluntary restraint agreement on exports to the Community under the Multifibre Agreements (q.v.).

Thomson, Lord (formerly George Thomson)
Former member of the Commission. Born Stirling, Scotland in 1921. During the Second World War served in the R.A.F. and subsequently became editor of the Socialist weekly 'Forward.' Entered politics in 1952 as Labour M.P. for Dundee East and after 1964 held the posts of Minister of State in the Foreign Office, Secretary of State for Commonwealth Affairs and Chancellor of the Duchy of Lancaster with special responsibility for European affairs. In this latter capacity he commenced the negotiations for British membership of the Community. Commissioner from 1973 to 1977 in charge of regional policy. Responsible for the Report on the Regional Problems in the Enlarged Community (Thomson Report (q.v.)) which led to the establishment of the European Regional Development Fund (q.v.).

Thomson Report
Report on the Regional Problems in the Enlarged Community named after the Commissioner in charge of regional policy and published by the Commission in 1973 at the request of the European Council (q.v.). It analysed the Community's regional problems and proposed Community action to supplement national regional policies, the coordination of existing Community measures in the regional field and an attempt to reduce the importance of the great industrial concentrations. This Report led to the establishment of the European Regional Development Fund (q.v.).

Thorn, Gaston
President of the Commission. Born Luxembourg in 1928 and educated at the Universities of Montpellier, Lausanne and Paris. Called to the Bar in Luxembourg, and entered politics as a Liberal member of the Luxembourg legislature in 1959. Served as member of the European Parliament from 1959 to 1969 during which period he was Vice-President of the Liberal Group and chairman of the Development Committee. Subsequently President of the Liberal International and the Federation of Liberal and Democratic Parties in the European Community. Minister of Foreign Affairs and Foreign Trade of Luxembourg from 1969 to 1980 and during this period served as President of the Council four times. Appointed President of the Commission in 1981.

'Three Wise Men, The'
A name given to Barend Biesheuvel (q.v.), Edmund Dell and Robert Marjolin (q.v.) whose report on European institutions appeared in 1979. They proposed a reduction in the size of the Commission so that each member country would have one Commissioner and greater powers for the European Parliament in the legislative process.

Threshold price
Calculated so that imported agricultural products are sold in the Community at the target price (q.v.), the difference between the world price and the target price being made up by a variable levy. The products covered are cereals, sugar, milk products and olive oil. *See also* Common Agricultural Policy.

Tindemans, Leo
Belgian political leader. Born 1922 at Zwijndrecht and educated at the Universities of Ghent and Louvain. Entered politics as a Social Christian in 1962 and held office as Minister of Community Affairs, Agriculture, Middle Class Affairs, the Budget and, since 1974, Prime Minister. In 1976 he produced an influential report on the further development of the European Communities (Tindemans Report q.v.). President of the European People's Party (q.v.) and recipient of the Charlemagne Prize (q.v.) in 1976.

Tindemans Report
Report on European union produced in 1976 by Leo Tindemans (q.v.), the Belgian Prime

Minister, at the request of the European Council. He proposed a way forward by giving greater powers to the Commission and to a directly elected European Parliament, by a common foreign policy, and by progress towards economic and monetary union, with the stronger members if necessary moving at a faster rate. Few of the member governments were enthusiastic about the proposals but, although no immediate action was taken to implement them, some have subsequently been realized.

Tobacco
Product regulated by the Common Agricultural Policy (q.v.). Norm and intervention prices are fixed annually for raw tobacco. Contract prices may be negotiated between producers and buyers and there is a refund for exporters consisting of the difference between Community and world prices. There is a Community proposal for the harmonization of excise duties on manufactured tobacco.

Togo
West African state signatory of the Yaoundé and Lomé Conventions (q.v.). Former French mandate which became independent in 1960.

Tokyo Round
World trade negotiations conducted under the auspices of the General Agreement on Tariffs and Trade (q.v.) between 1973 and 1979. The aim was to build on the achievements of the Kennedy Round (q.v.), and although the Community is not formally a member of G.A.T.T. the Commission was empowered to conduct negotiations on behalf of the Community as a whole. Agreement was reached on tariff reductions to be spread over a period of eight years during which the Common External Tariff (q.v.) will go down on average from 9.8 to 7.5 per cent. There is also a series of codes on standards, subsidies and duties and acceptance by G.A.T.T. of the principles of the Common Agricultural Policy (q.v.) in return for improved access to Community markets. The agreements came into force in January 1980, but negotiations continued on the selective application of trade safeguards by developing countries.

Tonga
Pacific island state signatory of the Lomé Conventions (q.v.). Former British protectorate which became independent in 1970 and is now a member of the Commonwealth.

Trade, technical barriers to
The E.C. is now an industrial free trade area and there are no restrictive barriers to the free movement of manufactured goods. There remain technical barriers relating to the specifications of the goods which may be imported into individual countries. These are imposed by national bodies responsible for standards and specify the health and safety regulations for each product. There are strict codes relating to such manufactures as motor vehicles, electrical equipment, domestic appliances and processed foodstuffs, and these often vary considerably among the member countries. Since 1969 the E.C. has been attempting to harmonize standards so as to bring about the elimination of technical barriers to trade. Acceptable norms have been reached in automobile safety, measuring instruments, electricity, chemicals, textiles and foodstuffs. It is aimed to produce a complete set of standards acceptable throughout the Community.

Trade Unions *see* European Trade Union Confederation

Transitional period
This is the period of time during which the provisions of the E.C. are implemented in stages. The first such transitional period was between 1958 when the European Economic Community came into existence and 1968 when the customs union became fully operational. Following the enlargement of 1973 there was a transition period of five years for Denmark, Ireland and the United Kingdom and another for Greece following her accession in 1981. The main elements progressively established during a transitional period are the customs union, free movement of labour, the financial contribution and enforcement of the regulations of the Common Agricultural Policy (q.v.). At the start of a transitional period a new member becomes immediately eligible for benefits under the common policies and financial instruments.

Transport policy
It is recognized that if free trade is to become in all ways a reality and distortions in competition are to be eliminated it is necessary to have a common policy on transport. This began with the implementation in 1955 of direct international tariffs for the transport of coal and steel products so as to ensure that the same price/distance relationship applied everywhere. Since then this principle has been extended into all forms of carriage in the Community and discrimination and tapering of charges to national frontiers have been made illegal. In road transport there has been harmonization of vehicle safety regulations (*see* Trade, technical barriers to) and of the permitted sizes of articulated lorries crossing intra-Community frontiers. International goods vehicle permits are granted on a quota basis and there are regulations on driving hours (*see* Tachograph). The proposal for an E.C. driving licence is now under consideration. In rail transport regulations have been agreed on the permitted subsidies for infrastructure and running costs, with the stipulation that aids must be transparent. In water transport there are regulations on barge sizes and the grading of canals, and similarly safety and pollution-prevention standards have been laid down for vessels entering Community ports. There are regulations on competition in the light of state subsidies especially with vessels from third countries. Similar action has been taken in the field of civil aviation and also in safety, simplification of formalities, mutual recognition of licences and environmental protection. The Community is actively involved in the improvement of the European transport infrastructure and particularly with the developing of transnational transport links. Community action has taken place in such areas as trans-Alpine communications, sea routes and cross frontier links both in planning and in the use of financial instruments such as the European Investment Bank (q.v.) and the European Regional Development Fund (q.v.).

Treaties of Accession, Paris, Rome *see* Accession, Treaties of; Paris, Treaty of; Rome, Treaties of

Triangle, The *see* Golden Triangle; Heavy Industrial Triangle

Trinidad and Tobago
Caribbean state signatory of the Lomé Conventions (q.v.). Former British colony which became independent in 1962 and is now a member of the Commonwealth.

Tripartite Conferences
Periodic meeetings of management, unions and Commission to discuss economic policy. The participation of both sides of industry in the policy-forming process at Community level. The aim is to appraise the overall economic situation and to define Community strategy in the areas of employment, prices, wages and finance.

Tugendhat, Christopher Samuel
Member of the Commission. Born 1937 in London and educated Cambridge University. Entered politics in 1970 as Conservative M.P. for the Cities of London and Westminster. Appointed Commissioner in 1977 with special responsibility for budget and financial control, financial institutions, taxation and personnel, and administration. Director of a number of companies and writer on business affairs.

Tunisia
North African state which is one of the signatories to the Maghreb (q.v.) cooperation agreements. Specific quotas are laid down for the export to the Community of certain products covered by the Common Agricultural Policy (q.v.).

Turkey
Eastern Mediterranean state signatory of an association treaty — the Ankara Agreement — with the E.C. in 1963. Over an agreed period, preferences were introduced for Turkish exports to the Community, and this concession was reciprocated. Preference ranges from complete abolition of customs duties to up to 50 per cent preference on certain agricultural products. Turkish agriculture was to be adjusted over a period of 22 years so that the provisions of the Common Agricultural Policy (q.v.) could apply to the country. The movement of workers was to be fully liberalized over the same period with no discrimination in employment, remuneration or social security benefits. A financial protocol was attached granting Turkey special European Investment Bank loans and this was renewed in 1973 and again in 1979. It

was visualized that the agreement would eventually lead to Community membership and Turkey is still anxious to bring this about. It is largely as a result of the poor performance of the Turkish economy that the establishment of a full free trade area has had to be delayed. Further problems have been the dispute with Greece and the country's political instability. Economic relations with the Community are close and the latter takes a half of Turkish exports and supplies over 40 per cent of imports. Turkish foreign policy has been to promote contacts with the Western nations and she is a member of both the North Atlantic Treaty Organization (q.v.) and the Organization for Economic Cooperation and Development (q.v.).

T.V.A. (Taxe à la Valeur Ajoutée) *see* Value Added Tax

U

Uganda
East African state signatory of the Arusha and Lomé Conventions (q.v.). Former British protectorate which became independent in 1962 and is now a republic within the Commonwealth. In view of the country's deterioration during the Idi Amin dictatorship (1971–1979) and the widespread economic distress following its collapse, special E.C. aid has been granted.

Union of Industries of the European Community (U.N.I.C.E.)
Organization of national employers federations within the Community with its headquarters in Brussels. It is regularly consulted by the E.C. and it monitors new legislation concerning company and financial matters and produces opinions on it for the Commission.

Union of Soviet Socialist Republics
The U.S.S.R. does not recognize the international legal status of the E.C. and there are no official bilateral relations. Economic contacts with Eastern Europe including the U.S.S.R. are conducted through the Council for Mutual Economic Assistance (Comecon) (q.v.).

Unit of Account *see* European Unit of Account

United Kingdom
Member state of the European Community since 1973. The United Kingdom of Great Britain and Northern Ireland has a total area of 244000 km^2 and a population of 56 millions. This produces a population density of 229 per km^2, which is well above the Community average of 170. Britain is a well established industrial country with the older industries (coal, steel, shipbuilding, textiles) mainly located in the north and west and the newer ones (vehicles, electrical goods, transport equipment) in the Midlands and south. The country was reluctant to enter fully into the original process of European unity and therefore did not initially join the European Coal and Steel Community or the European Economic Community. This was because she saw herself as being essentially a global rather than a European power and had close ties with the Commonwealth (q.v.) which she regarded as her proper sphere of activity and which was still responsible in the mid 1950s for a half of her overseas trade. A limited accommodation was reached with certain European countries through membership of the European Free Trade Association (q.v.) in 1959, and as her former colonies achieved independence Britain's role as a global power diminished. At the same time Commonwealth trade began to decline and Britain's economic strength to diminish. This was the background against which membership of the Community was sought in 1961 – 1963 and again in 1967. Attempts to bring the British and E.C. positions into line were unsuccessful largely because of French fears that British entry would dilute the Community ideals. The final negotiations which begun in 1969 were successfully concluded in 1972 and Britain became a member

in the following year together with Denmark (q.v.) and the Republic of Ireland (q.v.). Membership reflected the changed international position of the country since by the early 1970s the colonial empire had virtually ceased to exist, the Commonwealth was no longer an effective international force and Commonwealth trade had shrunk to 14 per cent of the country's total. In contrast to this, trade with the E.C. has steadily increased and by the early 1970s had reached one-third of the total. In spite of this, Community membership has remained a controversial issue in the United Kingdom, largely because the promised economic benefits failed to materialize and the country's relative position continued to decline. A contributory factor in this was the economic crisis of 1973 – the oil crisis – which plunged the whole western world into recession. However, the Referendum (q.v.) on membership held in 1975 produced a large majority in favour of staying in, but the country's chronically poor economic performance continued to raise doubts. Although possessing important physical resources and being self-sufficient in energy, the country has severe problems. These centre on a general industrial decline, failure to achieve adequate exports of manufactured goods and the existence of large problem regions in the north and west. Britain has been a major recipient of aid from the European Regional Development Fund (q.v.) and the European Investment Bank (q.v.) but she has still been a net contributor to the budget. This is largely due to her small but efficient agricultural sector which has not attracted subsidies under the Common Agricultural Policy (q.v.). There is also the high level of food imports from third countries the price of which has been artificially increased to bring them into line with Community prices. It is against this background that the United Kingdom has been an uneasy Community member, but in spite of this, successive governments have reiterated their intention to keep Britain 'in Europe.'

United Nations Conference on Trade and Development (U.N.C.T.A.D.)
Established in 1964 as a permanent organ of the United Nations. The aim is to facilitate the development of the world economy along lines most favourable to the developing countries and to ensure the provision of aid to these countries. Meetings take place every four years at which the Community participates as an observer. It is also a permanent observer at U.N.C.T.A.D.'s Trade and Development Council. The Community has broadly accepted the principles laid down by U.N.C.T.A.D. on trade with the developing countries and E.C. members have partly or completely cancelled the debts of the poorest of the developing countries. The Community has also accepted the resolutions of U.N.C.T.A.D. V (Manilla 1979) on direct aid to the least developed countries, condemnation of protectionism by the industrial countries, the need for structural adjustments and an integrated programme for the marketing and processing of raw materials. *See also* Lomé Conventions and North–South Dialogue.

United States of America, E.C. relations with
The only formal trade agreement between the E.C. and the United States was signed in 1977 and concerns fisheries off the American coasts. Consultations take place regularly at the highest levels between the two. Both subscribe to the Kennedy and Tokyo rounds of the General Agreement on Tariffs and Trade (q.v.) and there are institutional contacts between most Community members and the U.S.A. within the frameworks of the Organization for Economic Cooperation and Development (q.v.) and the North Atlantic Treaty Organization (q.v.).

Upper Volta
West African state signatory of the Yaoundé and Lomé Conventions (q.v.). Former French colony which became independent in 1960.

Uri, Pierre
Born 1911 in Paris and educated at the Ecole Normale Supérieure in Paris and at Princeton University. Economic Director of the European Coal and Steel Community from 1951 to 1959 and economic adviser to the European Economic Community from 1959 to 1961. Subsequently a member of the Experts Group on Long Term Development and the Competitive Capacity of the E.C. Writer on political and economic affairs.

Uruguay
South American state having non-preferential commercial agreements with the E.C. which are renewable annually. There is a principle of non-discrimination in imports and exports and special provisions are in force over the export of foodstuffs to the Community.

V

Value Added Tax (V.A.T.)
Method of indirect taxation employed in all member states of the European Community. The tax is levied on the difference at each stage between the sale price of the output of goods and services and the cost of the input of goods and services from primary production to final consumption. It was chosen by the E.C. in 1967 as a first stage in the eventual complete harmonization of all taxes and duties in the member states. It was considered to have the advantage of being neutral in regard to the origins of goods and services and to be an encouragement to production and modernization. Standard rates of the tax within the Community vary from 8 to 20 per cent, but it is aimed to bring them all into line so as to eliminate distortion of the conditions of competition resulting from different taxation levels. A Council decision stipulated that as from 1975 up to one per cent of all V.A.T. revenue was to be allocated to the Budget (q.v.). *See also* Excise Duty.

Vedel Report
Proposals by a working party appointed in 1971 by the Commission and chaired by Professor Georges Vedel to investigate the role of the European Parliament. It expressed the opinion that the Council had become 'the sole effective centre of power in the system' and it advocated greater powers for Parliament as a counterweight to this. It proposed that Parliament should have a suspensive veto, that its powers over the budget should be extended, and that the Commission should be obliged to consult with it on new proposals before submission to the Council. There should be a programme for direct elections to be introduced over an agreed period with a uniform voting system. The Vedel proposals had much support and a number of its recommendations have since been implemented. *See also* European Parliament.

Vegetable oils and fats
There are measures to regulate prices and production in the European Community of olive oil, oilseeds, soya beans, linseed, castor beans and cotton seeds. Target and market prices for olive oil are fixed annually and the difference between the two is the extent of aid to the producers. There is a levy on imports when prices fall below threshold price (q.v.) and special safeguards for imports from third countries in the Mediterranean area. Export refunds and subsidies to producers are based on total oil output. Target prices are fixed annually for colza, rape seed and sunflower seed, and aid to producers is based on the differences between target and world prices. For soya beans, linseed, castor beans and cotton seed, aid is per hectare harvested and based on target prices and yields fixed by the Community.

Vegetables *see* Fruit and vegetables

Veil, Simone
First President of the directly elected European Parliament. Born 1928 in Nice of a Jewish family and imprisoned during the Second World War. Subsequently entered the French civil service and became an administrator in the Ministry of Justice. Appointed Minister of Health in 1974 and introduced important reforming measures in health and social security. Elected to the European Parliament in 1979 becoming a member of the Liberal and Democratic Group. As President she is actively engaged in extending Parliament's role, particularly in the fields of policy making and budgetary control. *See also* European Parliament.

Vocational training
There are agreed Community principles on the coordination of training standards and the priority of regional and agricultural training schemes. The Community is involved in facilities for career guidance, exchanges of young workers, adult training and employment policies. To these ends a European Vocational Training Centre has been established in Berlin and a European Foundation for the Improvement of Living and Working Conditions (q.v.) in Dublin.

Vouel, Raymond
Former member of the European Commission. Born 1923 in Luxembourg and held posts in journalism and administration before joining the Luxembourg government in 1964. Held the posts of State Secretary for Public Health, Employment and Social Security, and the Mining Industry, and Minister for Finance and Land Development. From 1970 to 1974 he was chairman of the Parliamentary Socialist Group. Member of the Commission from 1976 to 1981 with special responsibility for competition policy.

Vredeling, Henk
Former member and Vice-President of the Commission. Born 1924 in Amersfoort and educated Wageningen Agricultural College. Entered politics as a Labour member of the Second Chamber of the Dutch Parliament in 1956 and served also as a member of the European Parliament. Appointed Commissioner in 1977 with special responsibility for employment, social affairs and the Tripartite Conferences (q.v.).

W

Water policy
Water is a vital resource for drinking, washing, bathing, industry and fisheries. Demand is constantly increasing and provision has to be made for security of supply and bringing new sources into use as required. A directive of 1975 laid down standards on the quality of drinking water and an agreement of 1979 harmonized methods of testing. Minimum acceptable standards for bathing water in rivers, lakes and coastal waters were also laid down in 1975. Pollution is now a major problem everywhere and much of it emanates from industry. This is something the Community is involved in by encouraging the member states to increase controls over discharge of dangerous substances and it has drawn up a 'black list' of these for guidance. Safety standards have been laid down for oil tankers frequenting the Community's ports. The E.C. is a signatory of the Barcelona Convention (q.v.) on the Mediterranean and is actively engaged in tackling the problems of the Rhine (q.v.) and its tributaries. The water policy is part of a wider concern for the environment and it increasingly relates to other areas of the Community's activity.

Waterways, inland *see* Transport policy

Werner Plan
Plan based on the reports of a committee on economic and monetary union chaired by Pierre Werner, Prime Minister and Minister of Finance of Luxembourg. The reports were presented in 1970 and were based upon agreements reached at the Hague Conference (q.v.) of 1969. They advocated that all decisions on economic and monetary policy should in future be taken at Community level. Economic and monetary union was to be implemented in successive stages from convertibility of currencies to fixing rates of exchange and freeing movements of capital. Out of this plan came the Snake (q.v.) and a closer coordination of economic policies. The Council also endorsed the plan's long term political implications.

West Berlin
This grew out of the four-power occupation of Berlin (q.v.) after the end of the Second World War. It came into being through the gradual amalgamation of the British, American and French sectors of the former German capital following the deterioration in relations between the West and the Soviet Union and their failure to reach an agreed solution to the problem of Germany. It became a non-Communist island in the middle of the German Democratic Republic (q.v.) and its political and economic isolation was sealed with the erection of the Berlin Wall by the Communists in 1961. Ties were increasingly forged with the Federal Republic of Germany (q.v.) and consequently with the European Community. Its total area is only 500 km^2 but its population of 2 million is still larger than that of any other German city. The Federal Republic of Germany's official policy has been to consider Berlin as the capital of the German nation and symbolic sessions of the Bundestag have been held there. It has been the recipient of German

and Community aid and has developed as a major centre of industry, research, education and the arts. Its legal status has been a matter of controversy between the Western powers and the Soviet and East German authorities and routes connecting it with the West have on occasion been closed or restricted. A compromise agreement signed in 1971 regularized its position and made way for closer contacts between West and East Berlin. The West Germans now regard it as a part of their territory and it has the status of a *land*. With certain provisos it is also considered a part of the Community and E.C. legislation and policies are applicable in the city.

West Germany *see* Federal Republic of Germany

Western European Union (W.E.U.)
International organization created in 1954 by France, Italy, the Federal Republic of Germany, the Benelux countries and the United Kingdom. It was established at the instigation of the British government to resolve the problems created by the failure of the European Defence Community (q.v.). The forthcoming full sovereignty of the Federal Republic of Germany aroused fears among the Continental countries and there was a desire for some form of acceptable international control. Under W.E.U. the new Federal Republic of Germany put its armed forces at the disposal of the North Atlantic Treaty Organization (q.v.), and Britain pledged herself to come to the defence of the other members if they were attacked and to continue to station troops on German soil. W.E.U. replaced the Brussels Treaty (q.v.) Organization and the Federal Republic of Germany was able to move on to full sovereignty.

Western Samoa
Western Pacific island state signatory of the Lomé Conventions (q.v.). Former New Zealand trust territory which became independent in 1962 and a member of the Commonwealth in 1970.

Wheat *see* Common Agricultural Policy

Wilson, Sir Harold
Former British Labour Prime Minister. Born 1916 and educated Oxford University. After little early enthusiasm for Europe, he came to the view that Britain should seek E.C. membership. During his first administration from 1964 to 1970 membership negotiations were initiated which were subsequently brought to a successful conclusion by the Edward Heath (q.v.) administration. Following Britain's accession, the second Wilson administration of 1974 to 1976 renegotiated the terms of entry. This was followed in 1975 by a national referendum (q.v.) on continued British membership and, following the government's official endorsement, there was a large majority in favour of remaining in.

Wine
Overproduction of this commodity in the Community has produced a considerable surplus and the existence of this wine 'lake' poses problems. In particular Italian competition has resulted in difficulties for French producers of ordinary wines. Under the Common Agricultural Policy (q.v.), premiums are made available for the conversion of surplus into industrial alcohol. Premiums are also available for the reduction of the structural surplus, in particular the conversion of vineyards in the Languedoc – Rousillon area.

Workers *see* Freedom of movement of workers

Y

Yaoundé Conventions
Signed in 1963 and 1969 at Yaoundé, capital of Cameroon, between the European Communities and the Associated African States and Madagascar (A.A.S.M.) (q.v.). All the Associates were ex-dependent territories and the majority of them had gained their independence since the signature of the Treaty of Rome (q.v.). There were initially 18 members of the A.A.S.M. but this became 19 with the admission of Mauritius in 1973. Each Convention lasted for a five year period and both made provision for the establishment of a free trade area between the Community and the A.A.S.M. The exceptions to this were certain products covered by the Common Agricultural Policy (q.v.), for which the Associates had favourable treatment in the Community market, and each Associate retained power to reintroduce protection unilaterally if it was considered necessary. Aid was also provided from the Community to the A.A.S.M., the agencies for this being the European Development Fund (q.v.) and the European Investment Bank (q.v.). Under Yaoundé I the total aid was 730 million units of account and under Yaoundé II it was 905 million u.a. This was non-refundable except for the 20 per cent of the funds emanating from the E.I.B. The Yaoundé II Convention was replaced in 1975 by the Lomé Convention (q.v.).

Yugoslavia
Non-aligned Communist state in Eastern Europe. Since 1970 Yugoslavia has had non-preferential trade agreements with the Community and an adjustment of the Common External Levy on beef and veal so as to encourage Yugoslav exports of these commodities. The Community is responsible for 26 per cent of total Yugoslav exports and 40 per cent of imports, and this situation has produced a large trade deficit. The country is attempting to promote closer relations with the Community.

Z

Zaire
African state signatory of the Yaoundé and Lomé Conventions (q.v.). Formerly the Belgian Congo it became an independent republic in 1960.

Zambia
State in southern Africa signatory of the Lomé Conventions (q.v.). Formerly the British colony of Northern Rhodesia it became independent in 1964 and is now a republic within the Commonwealth.

Zimbabwe
State in southern Africa signatory of the Lomé Convention (q.v.). Formerly the British colony of Southern Rhodesia, it declared its independence unilaterally in 1965 taking the name of Rhodesia. Following civil war and a brief return of British rule, it became Zimbabwe in 1980 and is now a republic within the Commonwealth. The European Community has an emergency aid programme to help the country's recovery.

Select Reading List

Broad, R. and Jarrett, R. (1972). *Community Europe Today,* Wolff, London.

Cohen, D. (1982). *Britain in the European Community,* Butterworths, London.

El-Agraa, A. M. (Ed.) (1980). *The Economics of the European Community,* Philip Allan, London.

Freeman, P. (Ed.) (1978). *Europe Today and Tomorrow,* Longmans, London.

Hodges, M. (Ed.) (1972). *European Integration: Selected Readings,* Penguin, Harmondsworth.

Mayne, R. (1970). *The Recovery of Europe: From Devastation to Unity,* Weidenfeld and Nicolson, London.

Morgan, R. (1981). *West European Politics since 1945, 2nd edition,* Butterworths, London.

Mowat, R. C. (1973). *Creating the European Community,* Blandford Press, London.

Parker, G. (1981). *The Logic of Unity. A Geography of the European Economic Community, 3rd edition,* Longmans, London.

Pryce, R. and Allen, D. (1982). *The Politics of the European Community, 2nd edition,* Butterworths, London.

Swann, D. (1978). *The Economics of the Common Market, 4th edition,* Penguin, Harmondsworth.

Vaughan, R. (1979). *Twentieth Century Europe: Paths to Unity,* Croom Helm, London.

Waterlow, C. and Evans, A. (1973). *Europe 1945 to 1970,* Methuen, London.